Get your HEAD OUT of the $AND!

every kiwi's guide to growing your money

Lisa Dudson

RANDOM HOUSE
NEW ZEALAND

A RANDOM HOUSE BOOK
published by
Random House New Zealand
18 Poland Road, Glenfield, Auckland, New Zealand
www.randomhouse.co.nz

First published 2005, reprinted 2010

ISBN 978 1 86941 735 2

Cover design: Katy Yiakmis
Printed in Australia by Griffin Press

Contents

Acknowledgements

No book can be completed without the support of others. Thank you to Tom Beran and the team at Random House for being so supportive when I approached them with the concept of *Get Your Head Out of the Sand.*

I would especially like to thank Mike Handcock, Clair Jones, Pauline Smith, John McConnell, Ron and Judith Dudson, Kerry Chalmers and Marlin Smith. They all kindly offered to be on 'reading duty', which provided invaluable feedback when I was fine-tuning my ideas. Also thanks to Vicki Watson for her help with the graphs.

Finally, thank you to all the clients I have worked with over the years. It has been incredible to witness the progress that so many of you have made in your lives.

Introduction

We live in a society in which we want everything *yesterday*. We know we should be more responsible with money and think about the long term, but there is always *tomorrow*. Through the media, various companies bombard us with their latest 'special offers'. They make it so easy for us, that consumer debt is now the norm. Today, the majority of New Zealanders simply don't have a good understanding of basic money-management.

So many of the people who come to see me are constantly worried about money – they are overwhelmed by all the information available, don't know who to talk to, and feel embarrassed because it's pretty basic stuff and they realise that they should know better. Unfortunately too many people put their heads in the sand believing it all to be too hard. Managing your money is consistently rated in numerous surveys throughout the Western world as one of the most unpleasant things in life – high up there with the death of a loved one, a divorce and public speaking. It is also one of the top two leading causes of relationship break-ups.

People can become so overwhelmed by their perception of the enormity of what needs to be done to sort out their finances that they just can't see the forest for the trees. The purpose of this book is not only to show you how you can improve your financial health, but also to help you realise that it might not be as bad as you think. Yes, there is some hard work involved – however, it's mainly a matter of consistently following some basic principles that will enable you to develop good money habits. People regularly talk to me about putting an investment portfolio together or buying an investment property, but the reality is that if they just got the basics right, in many cases they would be far better off.

Our current education system does little to help, and provides almost no financial tuition for our children. Robert Kiyosaki, probably the most well-known financial educator in the world, is constantly telling us how important it is for everyone to have a good financial education. On the positive front, the government seems to be taking some much-needed steps to bring more financial literacy into the curriculum. In the meantime, we all need to take responsibility for developing our own financial curriculum.

How to use this book

The book is divided into two main sections. The first deals with your mindset. There is an enormous amount of research out there demonstrating that success is very strongly linked to our attitudes. Teaching people how to become financially successful is not the difficult part – the challenge lies in creating the right attitudes, the motivation and disciplines required. The second part of the book focuses on the 'how-to' and takes you through the key areas of money-management. There are also a number of exercises located throughout each section, which I strongly encourage you to work your way through.

My passion in life is to make a difference in as many people's lives as possible through putting them in a stronger financial position to enable them to have more choices. For me personally, being in a position from which I can choose what I want to do and lead my life the way I desire is enormously rewarding. My aim is for you to have that same sense of freedom and choice as well.

The focus of this book is on achieving financial freedom in the sense of developing good money-management habits to enable you to gain control of your finances so that you are not constantly worrying about money. I am frequently overwhelmed by the enthusiastic feedback I receive from people I have worked with, who have attended one of my courses or heard me speak, so I know how well it works!

Let me share that money-management knowledge with you.

1

Live the life you desire

Go confidently in the direction of your dreams.
Live the life you have imagined.

Henry David Thoreau

All men who have achieved great things
have been great dreamers.

Orison Swett Marden

The future belongs to those who believe
in the beauty of their dreams.

Eleanor Roosevelt

Your images lead your reality.

Terry Orlick

Belief is the mother of reality.
Excellence is a state of mind.

Terry Orlick

Find your carrot

This may seem an unusual heading to start a chapter with. What I mean by this is, in order for us to have the life we desire, we must first find out what that life is. All of us dream of success and wish to see our desires fulfilled. However, few of us ever achieve our dreams. Why is this so? Basically, it is because there is a big difference between wishing for something and having an intense burning desire to achieve it. Sadly, most people dream about but don't pursue their goals. Those who do achieve their goals not only know what they want, they believe they deserve and can accomplish their dreams and they pursue them wholeheartedly.

Becoming financially free has very little to do with having great skill and knowledge in investing. I strongly believe that if you get the basics right – in other words all the things I am going to cover in this book – and start as young as possible you will become financially free. Financial freedom can mean different things to different people and it is an often-talked-about concept. It can mean anything from feeling in control of your finances to not having to work because your investments provide enough income for you to do what you want.

Interestingly, most people don't come to see me because they want to have a predetermined amount of money; they come to me simply because they have a number of things they want to do in their lives. They don't simply want to look at their bank balance and say 'I've got a lot of money'. Money is purely a tool for them to do the things they want, to live the life they desire.

Nevertheless, the most difficult thing I find with helping people with their finances is getting them to actually do what they need to do. It's relatively straightforward for me to teach someone the technical side of how to achieve financial freedom; the challenging part is keeping people on track. Things like motivation, focus, hard work, patience, determination, desire, discipline, and so on keep getting in the way! That's why it is important for you to find your carrot – to identify what dream or vision will keep you focused.

The success formula

30% knowing exactly what you want

+

35% positive self-image

+

30% I can do it

+

5% the how-to/technical

=

SUCCESS

Discover your vision

I have always believed that the best way to achieve what you want is to begin with the end in mind. Many people want to rush in and start the 'doing' straight away. However, you need the dream or vision to provide you with the motivation to keep you going. This dream or vision is the most important thing – it must come first. Dreams are all about love (the life you love, the people you love). Determining your personal dream, however, is not easy.

One of the greatest dreamers of the twentieth century was Walt Disney. He created the first sound cartoon, the first all-colour cartoon and the first animated feature-length motion picture. However, Disney's greatest masterpieces of vision were Disneyland and Walt Disney World. The spark for that vision came from an unexpected place.

Back when Walt's two daughters were young, he used to take them to an amusement park in the Los Angeles area on Saturday mornings. His girls loved the outings as much as he did. Walt was especially captivated by the carousel. He was enticed by the bright images racing around to energetic music.

> *But when he got closer, he could see that his eyes had been fooled. The horses were shabby specimens with cracked and chipped paint and only the ones on the outside row moved.*
>
> *However, the cartoonist's disappointment inspired him with a grand vision. He dreamed of an amusement park where the illusion didn't evaporate, where children and adults could enjoy a carnival atmosphere without the seedy side that accompanies some circuses or travelling carnivals. His dream eventually became Disneyland.*

For Disney, vision was never a problem. His innate creativity and desire for excellence made him always focus on what *could* be. Your own vision doesn't need to be quite so grandiose – it could be something as simple as being in control of your finances, getting to the end of the month with money left over, or being able to take yourself or your family on a holiday every year.

When he was only 12 years old, Henry Ford had an experience that was going to transform his life:

> *The biggest event of my early years was meeting with a road engine about eight miles out of Detroit one day when we were driving to town. I was then 12 years old . . . I remember that engine as though I had seen it only yesterday, for it was the first vehicle other than horse-drawn that I had ever seen . . . The engine had stopped to let us pass with our horses and I was off the wagon and talking to the engineer before my father, who was driving, knew what I was up to . . . It was that engine which took me into automotive transportation. I tried to make models of it, and some years later I did make one that ran very well, but from the time I saw that road engine as a boy of 12 right to today, my great interest has been in making a machine that would travel the roads.*

This chance encounter was obviously a turning point in Henry's life. The idea of building a machine that would travel the roads was going to haunt and obsess him from that moment on. Unfortunately, there is often a big gap between getting an idea and putting it into action. It is this gap that frightens many people off and condemns them into inaction.

Identify your vision

- ◇ What do you get excited about?
- ◇ What makes you happy?
- ◇ What do you want to spend your time doing?

What is important to you?

What matters to *you* is the only thing that matters. Don't worry about what everyone else thinks is important. We waste far too much time and energy worrying about what other people think we should do, think, and behave like. I'll say it again – what matters to *you* is the only thing that is important!

Okay, I appreciate that all this may seem a little intangible to you. Maybe you are sitting there thinking that this is just too hard, too complex and you can't get your head around it. But all you have to do to start with is spend some time on your own and write down your answers to the questions on pages 12 to 17. Don't overanalyse the questions, just jot down the first things that come into your head. Then get together with a friend or your partner and discuss them.

Ideally, from this exercise you will obtain a picture in your mind of what you want to achieve in your life. If you find the exercise difficult, just remember to try and keep your answers as simple as you can. You could try just writing down what your perfect week would look like and work from there. Personally, I find it a little difficult to get specific about what I want long term as so much happens in my life. However, I do have a long-term vision and I am very clear about how I want my week to look and the things I want to do in the year. For example, the amount of holidays and travel, time for exercise, friends, family, training and development, business and financial goals, and so on.

What gets you excited?

....

....

....

What makes you happy?

....

....

....

What do you think and talk about most of the time — what you want or what you don't want?

....

....

....

Who do you want to have around you?

....

....

....

What do you love to do?

....

....

....

What do you want to achieve in your lifetime?

....

....

....

....

....

Where do you want to live?

....

....

What type of lifestyle do you want?

....

....

....

....

....

If you won Lotto tomorrow, what would you change in your life?

....

....

....

....

....

If your doctor said you had six months to live, what would you do?

....

....

....

....

If you had five years to live, what would you do?

....

....

....

....

If you had unlimited money, what would you like to do?

....

....

....

....

What would your ideal day look like?

....

....

....

....

....

....

Write your own epitaph. What would you like people to say about you at your funeral?

....

....

....

....

....

....

What are the activities that give you your greatest sense of meaning or purpose in life?

....

....

....

....

....

....

What do you like to do on your weekends?

....

....

....

....

....

....

How much time would you want to take off every year and what would you like to do with this time?

....

....

....

....

....

....

How much time would you like to spend with your partner, children, family or friends?

....

....

....

....

....

....

What activities would you like to do with them?

....

....

....

....

....

....

What hobbies or sports would you like to do in your week and how much time would you like to spend on them?

How would you organise your year if you had no limitations and complete control over your time?

> ***Did you know?***
>
> The Chinese symbol for crisis is the same symbol used for opportunity.

You are what YOU believe

We create our own reality through what we think. The chances are if you are confident that you will succeed then you will. If you think you can't succeed, then you won't because you will be focused on failure.

Your external experiences always reflect your inner beliefs. If you heighten your belief in yourself you will have the ability to do greater things. To move forward in life you must change your beliefs. For Henry Ford, the word 'impossible' simply did not exist, as the following quote attests:

> *I refuse to recognise that there are impossibilities. I cannot discover that anyone knows enough about anything on this earth definitely to say what is and what is not possible . . . If some man, calling himself an authority, says that this or that can not be done, then a horde of unthinking followers start the chorus 'It can't be done.'*

Create a positive attitude

Both positive and negative influences on our thoughts, attitudes and behaviours can come from anywhere. Our partners, family, friends, work colleagues, the media, mentors and role models can all have an effect on the choices we make. It is important to be able to identify where the different influences in our lives are coming from and to make sure we absorb the positive but discard the negative.

Does anyone you know laugh when you talk about starting a budget, tell you that you don't deserve something, think you're nuts when you talk about your dreams? It's very frustrating to me to think about the number of times I come across people who are unsupportive and negative towards others. The effect of negativity in our lives is quite significant. My advice to you is establish *where* it comes from and go out of your way to either stay out of the paths of those who are negative or learn to pay no attention to their discouraging comments.

The tremendous power of affirmations

Affirmations are positive thoughts. Many successful people swear by the power of affirmations. Positive affirmations effectively stop negative programming. They flush out negative past conclusions that clutter your subconscious and build new constructive thought patterns. Affirmations must be positive, worded as clear, specific commands to the subconscious mind and only work if you *believe* they can work.

Winner of Ernst & Young's 2002 Young Entrepreneur of the Year award, Hamish Conway, repeated his affirmation about winning the award in the shower every day for a year before he won. He believed he would win and visualised receiving the award. He believes that his affirmations played a significant part in his achievement.

Here are some examples you could use:

- ◊ I can achieve anything I put my mind to.
- ◊ I am really good at managing my personal finances.
- ◊ I always spend my money wisely.
- ◊ I deserve happiness and success.
- ◊ I only think positive, healthy and happy thoughts.
- ◊ I believe strongly in my own judgements.
- ◊ I always earn more than I spend.
- ◊ I choose to live a positive life.
- ◊ My self-confidence increases every day.
- ◊ I look forward to enjoying each day.

You have choices

The truth is that everyone has choices in life. You need to realise that no one controls your life except *you*. There are times when you may not be fully in control of the circumstances that confront you, but you are certainly in control of your thoughts, how you choose to look at situations, and certainly how you choose to feel about them. The thoughts you choose to entertain every second of your life determine the results you will experience. If you choose to think happy, prosperous, healthy thoughts, you will naturally experience happy, healthy feelings. This positive mental state will help you deal with the challenges you will face on your journey.

In order for all of us to be successful in achieving the life we desire we must have a dream, we must have a desire to have the lives we want. Throw in belief in yourself and a good healthy attitude, the determination to keep taking a small step each day, a little bit of technical know-how and you *will* achieve what you want.

In a nutshell

- ☆ Find your carrot by discovering your vision.
- ☆ Establish what is important to you and what the life you desire is.
- ☆ Always believe in yourself.
- ☆ Have a happy, positive mental attitude.
- ☆ *You* have the power to make decisions to control your own destiny.

2

Myths, fantasies and excuses

Most people look for pleasing methods
not pleasing results.

Anon.

No one can make you feel inferior
without your consent.

Eleanor Roosevelt

Exceptions are the enemy of excellence.

Anon.

Where the mind goes, everything follows.

JoAnn Dahlkoetter

There are no problems – only challenges.

Anon.

Money attitudes and beliefs

Many of our beliefs and attitudes were developed when we were very young. We watch and learn our lessons from our parents, other family members, friends and teachers. Usually we don't realise what we have picked up along the way and, unknowingly, *their* beliefs and experiences begin to become our own.

While money-management skills can be quite easily learnt, attitudes and behaviours are often more difficult to tackle. They can result from deeply ingrained beliefs or experiences. It's important for you to realise what beliefs you have around money so that you can establish which ones you need to work on changing.

Money fantasies

Most of us will have some kind of fantasy about money lurking in our subconscious somewhere. Your brain can trick you into believing these fantasies could actually happen. However, if we really thought about them it would become clear how silly they really are. Do any of these pipe dreams sound familiar?

- ◊ *Lottery Living:* You actually believe you might nab a winning ticket, and you believe this every week.
- ◊ *I'm Gonna Marry a Millionaire:* And that single-minded focus keeps you both single AND broke. A man (or a woman for that matter) is not a financial plan.
- ◊ *Waiting for a Windfall:* Miscellaneous hopes for an inheritance, a bank error in your favour, a pot of gold in the back of the garage, and so on.
- ◊ *Unrealistic Expectations:* Thinking someone is going to pay you waaaaay more than they should, and that you'll retire in two years.
- ◊ *Sudden Success:* You'll sell that screenplay or invent a new kind of peanut butter that will make you a gazillionaire.

- *Do What You Love, The Money Will Follow:* The title of an actual book that has created financial disaster for everyone.
- *Ignorance is Profitable:* The crackpotted notion that by not paying attention to your money . . . one day you'll wake up RICH!
- *Things Have a Way of Working Out:* When clearly they don't if you don't do anything about it.
- *I'll Do It Later:* Time has an uncanny ability of disappearing and you wake up 30 years down the track still chanting to yourself you have plenty of time and will do it later.
- *Money is Not Everything:* Try living without it for a month.
- *Denial:* I am not that out of shape.

Right now you are probably laughing at the above list. But I am sure that if you think about it, at some point in time at least one of these thoughts has gone through your head, or you have heard someone else express them. Sometimes people make these comments in jest to either themselves or others, but I wonder what is really going on in their heads.

Did you know?

That 90% of what we worry about never happens.

The 'what ifs and buts disease'

So many people suffer from the 'what ifs and buts disease', otherwise known as 'excusitis'. We can always find an excuse about why we shouldn't be doing something. That little chatterbox that sits inside our head is both very active and powerful. You need to think sensibly about whether what it comes up with are actually good reasons or simply more excuses for you not to take action. Here are some of the most common excuses I have come across over the years:

The 9 most common excuses

① I wasn't taught in school; my parents didn't teach me about money

Okay, most of us weren't taught about money when we were young. It's a real issue I think we have with the school system in New Zealand. But that is the reality. There are lots of books, seminars, courses and experts out there that can help us learn about managing our money.

② I don't earn enough

The Millionaire Next Door, written by Tom Stanley and William Danko, which sold millions of copies around the world, provides some fascinating insights into the average millionaire. Although it's based on American millionaires I believe it holds true for most millionaires in New Zealand too. Here are some of the findings from the years of research they undertook:

- ◊ The average net worth of a millionaire is $3.7 million.
- ◊ The average millionaire lives in a house whose current value is $320,000. Over half have lived in the same house for more than 20 years.
- ◊ The average millionaire's taxable income is $131,000 a year.
- ◊ For the most part, millionaires describe themselves as 'tightwads' who believe that charity begins at home.
- ◊ Most millionaires drive older American-made cars. Only a minority drive new cars or ever lease their cars.
- ◊ Of half the millionaires surveyed the most they had ever paid for a suit or piece of clothing for themselves or anyone else was $399.
- ◊ They are dedicated investors – on average they invest nearly 20% of their income every year.

Getting ahead financially is not about how much you earn, it's about where you spend your money and living beneath your means.

③ It's my job to look after the kids; my partner's job is the finances

Money is a huge part of our lives. Love is what makes our lives special, but without money our lives can be quite difficult. The issue with this is that we have a growing single population – people are getting married later, divorce rates are high, and one partner often outlives the other. There is a fairly good chance that you will be alone for some part of your adult life. If your partner is good with money and you aren't, you may decide that they take day-to-day responsibility for your finances. However, at a minimum, it is essential that you are aware of what they are doing.

④ I don't understand these things, I don't have the brains to understand

> *Talent is overrated – Dr Benjamin Bloom of the University of Chicago conducted a five-year study of leading artists, athletes and scholars. It consisted of anonymous interviews with the top twenty performers in various fields, including pianists, Olympic swimmers, tennis players, sculptors, mathematicians and neurologists. That information was supplemented by additional interviews with those people's families and teachers. Bloom and his team of researchers sought to find clues to how these high achievers developed. What they discovered was that drive and determination –* not talent *– led to their success.*

I totally believe that everyone, given some effort on their part, has the ability to understand basic money principles. You do not have to be a financial wizard to be a good money-manager.

⑤ I don't have enough time,
there are never enough hours in the day

Time-management is a common problem. Most people today are time-poor. Have a look at your day and ask:

- ◊ How do I spend it?
- ◊ What ruts have I gotten myself into that I could easily break out of?
- ◊ What poor habits are eating valuable minutes of my life every day?
- ◊ Constantly ask: 'Is what I am doing now a good use of my time?'
- ◊ What impact can a few minutes make? Take a look at this. What if you were able to save:

  5 minutes by streamlining your morning routine (taking less time to dress, shave, put on make-up, drink coffee, read the paper and so on)?

  10 minutes by eliminating the things you do each morning to stall starting your work day?

  5 minutes by avoiding idle talkers or other distractions?

  10 minutes by taking a shorter lunch or break time?

Now those 30 minutes don't seem like much. But if you did those things every day, five days a week, for 50 weeks, you would gain an additional 125 hours of time every year. That's equivalent to about three 40-hour weeks to use for anything you want!

⑥ I am overwhelmed by too much information

The amount of information demanding our focus increases every year.

Today, in a weekend paper from any large city there is more information than the majority of the people living in the 1700s would have had access to in an entire lifetime. Most of us today feel overwhelmed by the information we receive. We may not be able to change the volume of information but we can change the way we handle it.

⑦ I want to wait until . . . I get my next pay rise/ next year/the kids go to school, and so on

We can always find a reason that can justify why we should put off doing something. The problem is that we often keep finding excuses to the point where it gets put off forever. Ask yourself honestly if it is just another excuse or it is a good reason.

⑧ I don't have the energy it takes

The potential energy we have in all of us is enormous. How many times have you done something that you procrastinated over for ages and then after you did it you said to yourself, 'It didn't take as long as I thought', or 'That wasn't as bad as I thought'? In the words of Thomas Edison: 'If we did all the things we were capable of doing, we could literally astonish ourselves.'

⑨ I am afraid of making a mistake and failing

Obviously, if you never *try* to do something – you will never *fail.* But then you aren't likely to succeed either. Success doesn't miraculously appear out of the blue. It's always a result of a concrete action and a positive mental attitude. Everyone fails at times, it is just part of life. The important thing is to learn from your failure and mistakes so that you eventually become successful.

You may have thousands of excuses but no good reasons

What are the myths and fantasies you have about money?

....

....

....

....

....

....

....

....

....

....

....

....

....

....

....

....

....

....

....

....

....

What are your common excuses? Are they just excuses holding you back, or are they good reasons?

Resolve to be responsible for your actions

The greatest enemies of success are negative emotions of all kinds. They can consume you, zap your energy and steal away your happiness. You need to learn how to remove negative emotions from your life. How many times have you woken up in the morning dreading your day ahead? Haven't you found that this attitude to the day follows you around and that you do indeed end up having a lousy day? What happens if you were to change that feeling to one of looking forward to your day? The likelihood is that you'll have a great day. Removing negative emotions from your life is an integral part of successfully taking control of it.

- Stop justifying things.
- Refuse to rationalise and make excuses for your behaviour.
- Don't worry about what other people think – what's important is what *you* think.
- Realise that *you* are responsible – not anyone else.
- Stop blaming others.
- Control your emotions and don't sweat the small stuff.

Resolve today that you will no longer dwell on myths, fantasies and excuses.

Did you know?

Albert Einstein experienced more failures than any scientist of his time; however, he also achieved more successes.

Create new positive money beliefs

Now that you have an understanding about what your beliefs around money are, you will know if you need to change the way you look at money. Do you feel comfortable with your current beliefs or do you need to develop some new and more positive ones? Some examples might be:

◇ I am in control of my money.

◇ What I don't know I feel comfortable that I can learn.

◇ I know that being financially comfortable gives me more choices in my life.

◇ If I plan my week I know that I will have time to manage my money.

◇ I know that managing my money is not that difficult – I just need to make a plan, take one step at a time, and stick to my plan.

Write down the way you would like to feel about money in the future:

....

....

....

....

....

....

....

....

....

(Note: you could refer to the affirmations in Chapter 1)

In a nutshell

- ☆ If you believe you are good with money, you will be good with money. It's a self-fulfilling prophecy.
- ☆ Don't concentrate on your failures with money to date, focus on what your money successes of the future will be.
- ☆ You may have thousands of excuses but no good reasons.
- ☆ Resolve today that you will no longer make excuses.
- ☆ Resolve today that you accept that you are responsible and you have the ability to change your beliefs.
- ☆ Money beliefs now = money beliefs of the future.

3

Success — one day at a time

Plan for the future because that's where
you are going to spend the rest of your life.

Mark Twain

You will never change your life until you change something
you do daily. The secret of your success is found
in your daily routine.

John Maxwell

A journey of a thousand miles begins with a single step.

Confucius

There are no short cuts to anywhere worth going.

Beverly Sills

We are what we repeatedly do.
Excellence then is not an act, but a habit.

Aristotle

What is success?

There is an old Chinese saying that *A journey of a thousand miles begins with a single step.* Many people have searched for success and never found it. They thought of it as the 'Holy Grail' or the 'Fountain of Youth'. Some thought of it as a possession to be earned or an object to be possessed. Success is none of those things. It is not a destination to be reached. It is a process – a journey to be taken. It's achieved one day at a time.

Success is being the person you want to be,
and living the life you want.

Success is completely an individual thing. We are very quick to look at others and think they are successful. Ironically, if you talk to these people you will often find that they don't think they are successful at all. This is because everyone measures success differently. The most important thing is to establish what success means to *you* – don't worry about what everyone else thinks.

So write down what success means to you. Some examples might be:

- Getting to the end of the month with $200 spare cash
- Being able to pay your bills on time
- Feeling in control of your finances
- Not fighting with your partner about money
- Getting to the point of having no personal debt.

Did you know?
Thomas Edison had made a thousand attempts before finally perfecting the light bulb.

Success to me means:

Success requires discipline

One of the best ways to improve your discipline is to do something you don't enjoy doing – *every day*. Successful people have achieved their goals because each day they have taken some small step towards their goals. Some of those steps may seem insignificant but they all add up. How many times have you read about how someone has been really successful at a sports event or their business has gone through extraordinary growth and you think, *Wouldn't it be great to achieve what they have*? What we fail to appreciate is that most of them have experienced a number of failures before their success. A successful business person may have had a dozen unsuccessful business ventures before one became a huge success. How many millions of times has a professional tennis player hit a ball? It's the lessons learned from the failures and the perseverance that in the end paid off. Once you were a baby learning to walk, every stumble eventually becoming a step. Please don't get too hung up on things that have not worked for you. Just accept that they have happened, learn from them and move on.

> Life *magazine named him the number one man of the millennium. The quantity of things he invented is astounding – 1093. He held more patents than any other person in the world, having been granted at least one patent every year for 65 consecutive years. His name was Thomas Edison. Most people credit Edison's ability to creative genius. He credited it to hard work. 'Genius', he declared, 'is ninety-nine percent perspiration and one percent inspiration.'*

Developing new habits

Thoughts lead to choices, choices lead to actions, actions lead to habits, habits lead to results.

Good habits are always created consciously, bad habits are always created unconsciously. Your goal is to develop good money-management habits that will be with you for a lifetime. Developing new habits can be challenging at first, but once they become habits you don't think about them, they are just part of who you are. Research shows us that it takes approximately 21 days to form a new habit. In the scheme of things that's not long. Keep persevering and you will have developed a new good habit before you know it.

Write down what you think your bad and good money habits are:

Bad Money Habits

....

....

....

....

....

....

....

....

Good Money Habits

....

....

....

....

....

....

....

....

Control the direction of your life

One of the great benefits of goal-setting is that it enables you to control the direction of your life. The starting point of achieving these goals is desire. As discussed in Chapter 1, you must develop an *intense burning desire* to have the life you want. Only then will you find the energy and the internal drive to overcome all the obstacles that will arise along your journey to achieving your goals.

> *For years, Monterey, California, was a pelicans' paradise. The town was the site of many fish canneries. Pelicans loved the town because the fishermen cleaned their catch, discarding the offal which the pelicans would feast on. They would be well fed without having to work for a meal. But as time went by, the fish stocks along the California coast became depleted and one by one the canneries were forced to shut down. That's when the pelicans got into trouble. Pelicans are naturally great fishers. They fly in groups over the ocean waves, and when they find fish, they dive into the water and scoop up their catch. However, these pelicans hadn't fished in years and had grown fat and lazy. Now that their easy meal had gone, they were actually starving. Environmentalists from the area racked their brains to figure out a way to help the pelicans and finally came up with an idea. They imported pelicans from another area and mixed them with the local birds. The newcomers immediately started fishing for their own food, and it wasn't long before the starving native birds joined in and started fishing for themselves again.*

The key message in this story is: Spend time with people you admire and learn from them.

There are NO short cuts

People often try to find short cuts to financial freedom. A few years back, I was invited to attend an investors' group. They were a bunch of people who were interested in investing and who would get together monthly to learn more about different investments, and to support and motivate each other. The group was engrossed in listening to one man describe this 'fantastic' investment from which he was getting a 10% per month compounding return, all for very little risk. I made a comment that it was unrealistic to expect this type of return and it must be a scam (note that he wasn't doing anything for this return other than sending money overseas). No one took any notice of me – I was just a financial planner who was only interested in selling managed funds. Anyway, the investment *was* a scam and he promptly went on to lose a significant sum of money. The amount of so-called 'smart, intelligent' people who have lost money in various scams is quite astonishing. Winning Lotto is probably the only scenario where you can make money overnight without any work and the odds of that happening aren't that flash! If it sounds too good to be true – it probably is.

Setting goals

Often our goals are visions of what we want long term. Most people I have seen over the years seem to find short-term goal-setting very effective. The strategy I recommend to my clients is to write down your short-, medium- and long-term goals in general terms, then break them down into a more specific annual plan, then into weekly or monthly tasks. Research shows us that people who set, work towards and achieve goals are more successful than those who don't. The people I know who are successful in achieving what they want in life are all good goal-setters.

> *Harvard University conducted a study between 1979 and 1989. In 1979, the graduates of the MBA programme at Harvard were asked, 'Have you set clear, written goals for your future*

> *and made plans to accomplish them?' It turned out that only 3% of the graduates had formulated written goals and plans. Thirteen percent had goals, but they weren't in writing. Eighty-four percent had no goals other than finishing their course and enjoying the summer. Ten years later, in 1989, the researchers interviewed the members of that class again. They found that the 13% who had goals that were not written down were earning, on average, twice as much as the 84% who'd had no goals. But most surprisingly, they found that the 3% of graduates that had clear, written goals when they left Harvard were earning, on average, 10 times as much as the other 97% of all graduates. The key message here is that the only difference between the groups was the clarity of the goals they had for themselves when they graduated.*

For goals to be effective and useful they need to be **SMART** goals: Specific, Measurable, Achievable, Realistic, and have a Timeframe. Each time you write down a goal, ask yourself these questions:

Specific – is your goal tailored and specific?

Measurable – can you measure your goal, is it quantifiable?

Achievable – do you think this goal is achievable if you are focused, committed and prepared to put in the effort?

Realistic – if you are honest with yourself, is your goal realistic for you to achieve?

Timeframe – a task will always expand to fill the amount of hours you devote to it, so allocate a timeframe.

Step One – Establish your goals

For you to be successful in achieving your goals you must write them down. I don't believe that having goals only in your head will work. Goals *must* be written down and put in a place where you regularly see them.

Write down your short-, medium- and long-terms goals.

short-term goals (1 year)

- ....
- ....
- ....
- ....

medium-term goals (2-5 years)

- ....
- ....
- ....
- ....

long-term goals (5 years +)

- ....
- ....
- ....
- ....

Examples of objectives

- provide a regular income for your family after your death
- invest money on a regular basis
- accumulate sufficient assets for retirement
- develop an investment plan
- replace your income if you become ill or disabled
- budget more effectively
- buy a new car
- travel
- fund children's education
- reduce tax
- eliminate/reduce debt
- provide a lump sum in the event of major illness

Step Two – Complete your personal annual planner

Now that you have outlined your short-, medium- and long-term goals you need to break them down into an annual planner.

Ask yourself these questions:

1. Are these short-term goals in line with your long-term ones?
2. Do these short-term goals take you closer to achieving your long-term goals?
3. Are they **SMART** goals?

Business/job/career *(e.g. work towards promotion, increase business turnover by 15% this financial year)*

- ....
- ....
- ....
- ....

Personal *(e.g. do a university paper, invite friends around for dinner every month)*

- ....
- ....
- ....
- ....

Health *(e.g. learn to play tennis, lose 5 kg)*

- ....
- ....
- ....
- ....

Family *(e.g. take partner/family away for a two-week holiday)*

- ....
- ....
- ....
- ....

Financial *(e.g. complete budget every month, increase mortgage payments by $200 p/m, pay off credit card)*

- ....
- ....
- ....
- ....

Step Three — Develop your task list

Now that you have established your goals, and worked out which ones you want to achieve this year, break them down into weekly or monthly manageable tasks. Use the template on the next page. It is designed so that it is simple to use, easy to complete and ideal to put on the fridge or somewhere you can see it regularly.

Step Four — Review your progress

I can not stress strongly enough how important it is to regularly review your progress – and it is most effective to do this weekly, especially when you are starting out. You may find that after a while it's okay to have these reviews less frequently – however, anything longer than a month and you may find yourself falling off the wagon. Most people experience more success if they carry out this review with a friend or partner.

No.	Task	By Whom	Due Date	Completed
1	Carry a notebook to track spending for a month	Mary/Tom	1 month	
2				
3				
4				
5				
6				
7				
8				
9				
10				

Tips for staying on track

- ◇ Realise you will not achieve your goals or aspirations until they become a priority.
- ◇ Set aside a regular time for your review – the same time each week/month is effective for most people.
- ◇ Make yourself accountable for your goals.
- ◇ Don't beat yourself up if you don't achieve all you set out to – instead, resolve to do better next week.
- ◇ Pat yourself on the back if you achieve the goals you set out to achieve.
- ◇ Create an agenda for your review and stick to it. It's amazing what you can achieve in a short time if you are focused.
- ◇ Don't spend too much time during your week thinking about how well you are doing – save it for your review time. You can waste a lot of time going around in circles overanalysing what you are doing.
- ◇ If you are in a relationship, share the tasks according to where your strengths lie.
- ◇ Support and encourage each other.
- ◇ Remember: one small step at a time.

When first starting this review process, you may find that it takes more time than you would like. It takes a bit of practice to get it right.

Jen and Mark, a couple in their 40s, came to see me to develop a financial strategy to help them accumulate funds for their retirement. Early in the consultation, it was clear to me that they first needed to develop some good money-management habits before they started setting up an investment plan. Together we worked out a number of things that needed to get tidied up and set out some tasks for them to accomplish. As with most couples, money had become a regular discussion topic and created a lot of stress in their relationship. They talked, or argued, about money over breakfast, on the way to do the shopping, during dinner, and so on. Money regularly seeped into their conversations, they never seemed to come to any conclusions, and it was driving them crazy. I suggested that they set aside a time each week to talk about their finances, review the previous week's tasks and goals and set new ones for the following week. I also suggested that they tried not to discuss their finances at any other time except during their review session. Jen and Mark came back to see me three months later. They said their weekly review sessions had proved invaluable. They no longer argued constantly about money and felt much better about their financial position. They had completed all their tidy-up tasks, created some new money habits and were in a much better place mentally about money. This demonstrated to me that not only were they ready to start their investment plan but also that they had the commitment to stick to it. Even more importantly, they had set up a lifetime habit of developing their long-term relationship with each other.

Review questions

Below are some questions you can ask yourself, or your partner/friend can ask you, each time you do your review. They may help to keep you focused:

What are the top two thoughts that limited your progress?

- ....

....

- ....

....

What are the top two things you are going to stop doing?

• ....

....

• ....

....

What are the top two things you are going to start doing?

• ....

....

• ....

....

What did you learn?

....

....

....

....

How can you be more effective?

....

....

....

....

What did you accomplish? What are the top two things that you did well?

....

....

....

....

On a scale of 0–10 what was your commitment level this week?
What do you want it to be next week?

This week .... *Next week* ....

Just do it!

The primary difference between high achievers and low achievers is *action orientation.* Those who accomplish a lot in their lives are very action-oriented. They are always busy, always moving, and when they have an idea they immediately take action on it. Remember, these actions don't need to be huge tasks. It is not necessarily the size of the steps or actions you take, it's the quantity and the consistency of them. For example, before you buy anything ask yourself if you really need it instead of just buying it. It will only take a moment, and if you do it enough times you will create a good money habit that could save you thousands over your lifetime. Resolve today to start taking those small steps each day towards achieving your goals.

SUCCESS

Select your goal

Unlock your personal potential

Commit yourself to your plan

Chart your course

Expect problems

Stand firm on your commitment

Start today

For things to change – first *I* must change

On the next page is a success formula I came across – from Mike Litman, co-author of the bestselling book *Conversations with Millionaires.*

I dislike going backwards and I'm passionate about progress.

One of my strongest beliefs is never go to bed the same person that you were when you woke up.

Learn something, do something, stretch yourself, you must GROW each day.

This is so important.
Make DAILY PROGRESS a strong belief you hold.

But here's something that is crystal clear in my life.

Do you want to get to the next level in your life and business?

Here's how I do it.

You see, there's always a CONSTANT, there's always something that must happen before you can move to the next level.
Every time I do 'this', I move to another level in what I'm pursuing.

Your next level always starts by making a DECISION.

Usually, this decision is a bit scary as well.

Most people's best friend is indecision and that's why their growth is slow — as slow as turtles walking across Main Street.

You MUST start making more decisions. (Read this again)

DECIDE today to start something new, do something that makes you a bit uncomfortable.

You should be doing AT LEAST one uncomfortable thing a day in your life or business.

Decide to MAKE YOUR MOVE.

Make a decision today and then do this: TAKE THE FIRST STEP.

That's it. Ask yourself this question:
What decision have I been putting off that if decided today could move my life and/or business forward?

Remember, you don't have to get it right, you just have to get it going.

In a nutshell

- ☆ Success is being the person you want to be and living the life you want.
- ☆ There are no short cuts.
- ☆ Develop new habits.
- ☆ Set SMART goals.
- ☆ Review your progress.
- ☆ Create a supportive environment to keep you on track.
- ☆ Just do it! Resolve today to start taking those small steps each day towards achieving your goals.

4

Your financial snapshot

The Lord gave us two ends: one to sit on
and the other to think with.
Success depends on which one we use the most.

Ann Landers

He is able who thinks he is able.

Buddha

The pessimist sees difficulty in every opportunity.
The optimist sees the opportunity in every difficulty.

Winston Churchill

A person who aims at nothing is sure to hit it.

Anon.

Establish your starting point

Do you really know where you stand financially? In order to get control of your finances and plan your financial future effectively, you need to first know where you stand today. How do you do that? Firstly you need to work out what your net worth is.

A net worth statement is a snapshot of your current financial situation, and it will give you important clues about where you should concentrate your financial planning efforts.

Your net worth is the difference between all the things of value that you own, and all the debts you owe. In financial terms, your net worth is your assets minus your liabilities. Effectively, if you sold everything today how much money would you have in your hand? Calculating your net worth is fairly simple to do.

Complete the template opposite and then add up the totals in each column.

Now subtract your liabilities from your assets. Is the number positive? If so, you have more assets than liabilities.

If you have more assets than liabilities, you have a positive net worth. This is a good thing. If the number is negative (more liabilities than assets), you have a negative net worth. This is not such a good thing, but it's information you need to know.

Did you know?

- The average net worth of a New Zealander is approximately $60,000
- 16% have a negative net worth
- 30% have a net worth over $200,000
- The most valuable asset is residential property, accounting for approximately 43% of total assets
- The largest debt is mortgage debt, which makes up approximately 80% of all debt

Source: 2001 Household Savings Survey – Statistics New Zealand

Net Worth Statement

Asset Item	*Value $ (asset)*	*Debt $ (liability)*
Principal Residence		
Holiday House		
Motor Vehicle (1)		
Motor Vehicle (2)		
Boat		
Investment Property (1)		
Investment Property (2)		
Investment Property (3)		
Investment Property (4)		
Vacant Land		
Forestry		
Business Interests		
Collectibles		
Superannuation		
Overseas Pensions		
Life Policies (cash value)		
Cash in Bank		
Managed Funds		
Shares		
Term Deposits		
Other Investments		
Credit Card (1)		
Credit Card (2)		
Loans to Family Members		
Loans to Others		
Student Loan (1)		
Student Loan (2)		
Hire Purchase (1)		
Hire Purchase (2)		
Overdraft		
TOTAL	$	$

Gerry, a tradesperson in his early 50s, had owned his small business for many years. He thought that with retirement just over 10 years away he needed to start putting together an investment plan. Once we had completed his net worth statement, we established that Gerry was worth over a million dollars. About half of that worth was his house, with the balance being mainly a number of small term deposits. Basically, whenever Gerry had some extra money in his business (he had always drawn a modest wage to live off) he had put it in a term deposit in the bank. Then the bank would send him the maturity notices, which he kept reinvesting. He had absolutely no idea that he had over $400,000 of them. On his current levels of expenditure, Gerry could retire immediately, and he'd thought he had to work for at least another 10 years.

Belinda and Peter, a young married couple in their late 20s, earning a combined income of around $150,000 pa, owned their own home and wanted to start a savings plan. However, once we completed their net worth statement, they had a negative net worth of approximately $35,000. They were both shocked, as they thought they were doing well. But they had only 5% equity in their home as they had taken out a 95% mortgage, on which they were only paying the minimum 25-year payments when they could actually afford much more. They both had loans on their cars, debt on their credit cards and a computer on hire purchase. They were living beyond their means but didn't realise what they were doing as they had never done a budget or totalled up what they owned and what they owed. This was certainly a big reality check for them and gave them the motivation to develop a budget so they could spend their money more wisely.

Managing your bank accounts

Often I find that people have a number of different bank accounts and are not sure why they have so many and what they are used for. One of the keys to good money-management is to keep things as simple as possible. Typically, all you need is one day-to-day account and one for savings. Complete the table on the next page to help you check on what you actually have.

Checklist for managing your bank accounts

- ◇ How much do you spend on fees each month? This needs to be added to your budget.
- ◇ Can you reduce your monthly fees?
- ◇ How many accounts do you have? Do you need all of them? A general rule of thumb is to have one for day-to-day expenditure and one for your savings.
- ◇ Does your bank offer any no- or low-fee accounts that you can link to your mortgage account?
- ◇ Are you using the Internet for your banking? Not only is it convenient but often the transaction fees are lower.
- ◇ Some banks offer no- or low-fee accounts to students, the unemployed, children and the elderly – are you entitled to any of these?
- ◇ Have you spoken to your bank to check that you have the right account to best suit your needs?
- ◇ Can you reduce the amount of EFTPOS or cheque transactions by taking out a cash amount at the beginning of each week?
- ◇ What interest does your savings account pay? Can you get a better rate?

Name of bank	Type of account	Fees paid each month	Interest paid each month	Balance of the account	Purpose of the account

> ***Did you know?***
> The secrets of the rich are not secrets.
> They are a set of money-management principles
> that millionaires adhere to.
> Not-so-rich people ignore them mainly because
> they are too impatient to become rich.

The dreaded notebook!

Now that you have established what your net worth is, you need to work out where your money goes each month. Before a realistic budget can be developed you need to understand exactly where your money is going – and I mean *exactly*. The vast majority of people have no idea how much money they spend each month or what they spend it on. They just know that they spend it all, and in a lot of cases they spend more than they earn.

An excellent way to track your spending is to carry around a small notebook or folded sheet of paper with you for one month and write down *every cent* you spend and what you spend it on. Moans and groans are the typical reaction I get when I mention this exercise. I appreciate that it's a bit of a nuisance, but even though people protest about it the feedback I get from those who do it is quite amazing. I have yet to come across anyone who was not surprised by the results and how much money they spend on things they didn't think about. Typically, it's discretionary items like meals out, takeaways, magazines, chocolate bars, clothes, and so on.

> Katrina, a professional woman in her mid-30s, knew she wasn't good with her money. However, until she went through the notebook exercise she had no idea how bad! On her income and expenditure form (which I get all of my clients to complete) she listed her net income as $7000 p/m and her expenses at $4000

p/m. I asked her if she had missed out listing her savings account on her net worth statement as I couldn't see where she was saving her extra $3000. I suggested she do the notebook exercise. Like most of my clients when I mention this exercise, she wasn't thrilled. However, she persevered and wrote down every cent she spent for a month. The reality was she was spending everything she earned and wasn't aware of where it was going. After we had established where her money was going we put together a realistic budget for her to work towards. After once dreading the idea of managing her money, today she is in a very strong financial position, has developed some good money habits and is confident that she will always be in control of her finances.

Sandy didn't earn a lot of money, she worked as an admin assistant and earned around $34,000 pa. She had no money left at the end of every month and thought she would never be able to get ahead financially and save a deposit for the house that she had always dreamed about. When we looked at what she spent her money on, there was around $350 p/m on lunches, takeaways and magazines. I suggested that if she borrowed magazines from her friends once they had read them, and limited her lunch and takeaway money to $50 each month, she could save the remaining $300 into a house deposit account. In order for this to work for her long term, she needed to be committed to her goal, to put the $300 into a savings account the day she got paid and keep working with a budget to make sure she could continue to afford the $300.

Once you have completed this exercise you will be in a position to establish a budget – or for those who feel they have a phobia about budgets, we'll call it a spending plan. More on this in the next chapter. Establishing your starting point is a crucial step in your journey to financial freedom. It isn't that often that I come across clients who have a clear understanding of what they are really worth. However, before you can achieve your goals you need to know what point you are starting from.

In a nutshell

- ☆ Establish your starting point by working out what your net worth is.
- ☆ How much do you *own* and how much do you *owe*?
- ☆ Get the best use out of your bank accounts.
- ☆ Work out where your money is currently going.

5

The big bad 'B' word: Budget

A budget is people telling their money where to go
instead of wondering where it went.

John Maxwell

We are what we repeatedly do.
Excellence then is not an act, but a habit.

Aristotle

It is easy for most of us to meet expenses
. . . we meet them everywhere we turn.

Anon.

Money is not everything,
but it's right up there with oxygen.

Brent King

One of the greatest discoveries a man makes,
one of his greatest surprises, is to find he can
do what he was afraid he couldn't do.

Henry Ford

Aligning your spending with your goals

This is probably the single most important financial skill for you to master. And the best news is that it's not that hard. It may not be that enjoyable, especially at first, but it's definitely not that hard.

You need to learn to spend on the things that you care about, and that help you get to where you want to be. It's about learning to stop mindless spending and learning to live below your means. Mindful spending is about buying what you want, not what you are *told you want.* Advertising is all around us. Millions of dollars are spent every year by companies finding ways to trick your mind into believing that their product is something you really need. Every dollar that you spend on things that you really don't need is a dollar further away from your dream and your goals.

Here are two very important questions to ask yourself when you are about to spend money:

1. Do I really *need* to have this item, or is it that I *want* it?

2. What are the consequences of spending this money?

Develop your spending plan

Without exception, you have to make a written plan. Quite simply, *managed money works harder.* There is no one-size-fits-all budget. It varies from month to month, so sit down and plot on paper how each dollar will be spent before the month begins. You will have all completed the notebook exercise from the previous month, so you will be able to develop your plan accurately.

Unfortunately, most budgets are doomed to failure. This is mainly because they are too much like a 'quick-fix diet plan'. They work well for a few weeks then it gets too hard and most people fall back into their old habits. Conventional budgets also fail to plan for emergencies, are unrealistic and too strict. Make sure you have made allowances for miscellaneous expenses that may arise.

The big budget myth

It doesn't matter whether you have a budget, a so-called spending plan, or some other strategy for managing what comes in and what goes out. Whatever money-management method you use, there's a tendency to imagine that it will run itself. You must be determined to stick to your budget.

Track what goes out

You need to develop the habit of saving automatically and spending selectively. I am not suggesting you live on baked beans but it is important to understand exactly *where* your money goes. It's all about living well on less. Where do you spend small amounts of money on a daily basis? For many, it's something as seemingly insignificant as a few dollars for a cup of gourmet coffee, but it all adds up. That doesn't mean you necessarily have to give up your latte break. You do, however, need to change your thinking. Notice exactly how much you are spending and where. Refer back to Chapter 4 regarding keeping a notebook for tracking this expenditure if you need to.

It's not about how much you earn

It doesn't matter *how much* you earn. Typically, the more you earn the more you will spend – you will expand your spending to fit your income. People moan and groan about never seeming to have any money. In most cases, if you look at your lifestyle carefully, there's almost always a way to trim costs and make do with less. Cutting costs, though, is more than a handful of good tips that you use when things get really tight – it's a way of life. Now, I am not suggesting you live like monks, but most of us spend money on things that we don't really need without even realising it.

> ***Did you know?***
>
> Money problems are one of the leading causes of relationship break-ups.

Ross and Jo were a couple in their late 20s earning almost $500,000 per year including bonuses between them. They had an excellent future ahead of them careerwise but they had no money. You may gasp, but they let their spending grow to fit their income. Their only asset, apart from their numerous 'toys', was their home. They had used one of their parents' house as security and taken out a 100% loan and almost two years later still had almost no equity because they had been making only the minimum payments. They believed their financial situation was fine and that they had plenty of time on their side. The problem is that with this kind of attitude to money they would most likely end up being the kind of people who came to see me in their mid-50s, stressed out from years of overwork, still with a big mortgage (probably on a much higher-value house) and with no savings to speak of.

Give yourself an allowance

Part of what we spend our money on is what we call discretionary items – such as clothes, make-up, entertainment, holidays, magazines, takeaways, and so on. This is where most people get into trouble with their spending. The most successful way that I have found to manage this discretionary spending is to give yourself a set amount each month to spend on these items. If you want to put all of it on a new dress or jacket, that's your decision, but the trade-off is that you can't buy anything else until you get next month's allowance. I find this concept works particularly well for couples, as often people have different opinions on where they want to spend their money. If you each have a set amount, you can spend it on whatever you like. The key thing is to stick to your limit and make sure your allowance is realistic.

Karen was 37, had a great job but credit-card debt of $30,000. She had no assets, was currently renting, though luckily she did earn around $90,000 a year. She was embarrassed about her financial situation and wanted to get on top of things so she could buy a house. Obviously, she was a big spender with most of it going on discretionary items. We went to work on developing a budget for her. She was willing to cut out or reduce most things except for her cosmetics. Now that may seem silly to many of you, especially the guys, but to her it was important. She wasn't willing to give those items up. That wasn't necessarily a problem as long as she stuck to her monthly allowance. However, unless you have iron willpower, if you cut out too much you are likely to fall off the wagon.

Planning for emergencies

Everyone should have an emergency fund, which is a sum of money (equivalent to 3–6 months of your expenses) put aside for a rainy day. This needs to be in an account where you can easily access the money if you have an unplanned expense. Beware not to rationalise the use of your emergency fund for something you should save for and purchase.

Things that boost your ego but deflate your wealth

There are a number of things that we buy that make us feel good, but the only other thing they achieve is to take us further away from achieving our financial goals. We need to give these types of purchases a lot of thought. They may include: new cars, the latest TV or stereo, new appliances, designer clothes and toys (e.g. jet skis, motorbikes). You need to ask: are these things taking you closer to your goals or further away? If the answer's further away, is it worth it?

Your spending plan must:

- ◊ be written;
- ◊ have a certain degree of flexibility;
- ◊ be reviewed regularly – ideally every week for the first three months.

If you don't see it, you won't spend it!

If you need to put money aside for a specific purpose like a holiday or investment, put it into a separate savings account with the understanding that it is for that purpose. It's easiest to get a specific amount direct-credited into your savings account each month as soon as you get paid so you won't be tempted to spend it. *Don't dip into it for other things.*

Don't worry about the Joneses

No doubt you have heard the saying 'Keeping up with the Joneses'. Don't be fooled by what you perceive other people to have. You will often find that the Joneses either can't do maths or are broke. I can confidently say that what you see is not usually as good as it seems. I have observed so many people over the years who have big salaries, nice cars, houses in the best suburbs and wear the latest designer clothes, but underneath it all they are struggling to get from one month to the next.

Mary came to see me a few years ago about investing in residential property. She knew she needed to do something as she and her husband Paul were both in their mid-50s with almost nothing set aside for retirement. Paul, along with some partners, owned a busy medical practice on which he still owed $150,000 for his share of the business loan. He was working very long hours and was exhausted at the end of each week. Mary knew that it was up to her to take control of their finances. The trouble was, they still had a small mortgage on their own home, a large mortgage on their holiday home, three children in private school, and leased cars. Even though she had meticulously done their family budget, the bottom line was they were living beyond their means. The only way forward was for either Mary to go back to work or for them to make some cutbacks.

Dealing with demanding children

One day at the gym I got talking to one of the instructors about managing money, after she had seen me reading a finance book while I was on the bike. We had a chat about the similarities between personal finance and health. Even though there is far more awareness today about how important it is to look after our health, obesity levels are on the rise every year, as are major health issues like diabetes. It had taken her husband being out of work for a couple of years for them to start becoming more careful of where they spent their money. Our discussion led on to how parents deal with the constant wants of their children. She had an anecdote for me: 'I took my two-year-old son to The Warehouse shopping one day when he exclaimed, "Mum, Mum, I need it, I want it, I love it, what is it?"' I asked her if she had given in. No, but she said that she probably would have if it had been the time before her husband was out of work. It really took a major change in their lives for them to realise that they were better off saying 'No'.

Don't be embarrassed — just take action

I recently had a conversation with someone who said to me: 'You're a financial planner, aren't you? I really need to come and see you. My wife and I are terrible with money. In the last few years we've been refinancing our house to give us money to live on. I know we should be doing something about it but we're so embarrassed about the mess we've got ourselves into.' Unfortunately, I am still waiting for that phone call to arrange an appointment. Please don't be embarrassed about your financial situation. There are lots of people who struggle to manage their money. The most important thing is to take some action and work towards becoming better at your money-management.

Plan templates

Pages 67 to 73 contain some templates that you may find useful. I suggest that for the first month you set aside 30 minutes each week to complete your budget. It may take less time than this, depending on how aware you are of where your money goes.

Income $	**Weekly**	**Monthly**	**Annually**
Salary/wages — combined after tax			
Interest/ dividends			
Other (bonus, tax refund)			
TOTAL INCOME	**a**	**a**	**a**

Payments Fixed $	**Weekly**	**Monthly**	**Annually**
Superannuation/savings			
Mortgage/rent			
Loan/hire purchase			
Cars — registration/ insurance			
Insurance — life/ disability (self/partner)			
Insurance — home/contents			
Insurance — medical/hospital			
Rates			
Electricity/gas			
Telephone			
Childcare/babysitting			
Fees — school/university			
Total Fixed Payments	**b**	**b**	**b**

Total Income (a) minus Total Fixed Payments (b) =

Surplus income after all expenses **c**

(continued)

Payments Variable $	Weekly	Monthly	Annually
Groceries/meat/ vegetables			
Clothing/ shoes			
Cars — service/ tyres/petrol			
Fares — train/bus			
Chemist/Dentist/ Doctor/Optometrist			
Newspapers/magazines/ books			
Home — painting/repairs/ garden			
Appliances/furniture — new/repairs			
Total Variable Payments	**d**	**d**	**d**

Total Surplus Income (c) less Total Variable Payments (d) =

Balance available for discretionary payments **e**

(continued)

Payments Discretionary $	**Weekly**	**Monthly**	**Annually**
Holidays			
Entertainment — restaurants/movies			
Cigarettes/alcohol/ work lunch/takeaway			
Sports/hobbies/ club fees			
Children's pocket money/ toys			
Hair care/ dry-cleaning			
Gifts — Xmas/ birthday			
Donations			
Other			
Sundry cash — self			
Sundry cash — partner			
Total Discretionary Payments	**f**	**f**	**f**
Surplus income after all expenses (e minus f)			

Income $	Jan	Feb	March	April	May	
Salary/wages — combined after tax						
Interest/dividends						
Other (bonus, tax refund)						
TOTAL INCOME						
Payments Fixed $						
Superannuation/savings						
Mortgage/rent						
Loan/hire purchase						
Cars — registration/ insurance						
Insurance — life/ disability (self/partner)						
Insurance — home/contents						
Insurance — medical/hospital						
Rates						
Electricity/gas						
Telephone						
Childcare/babysitting						
Fees — school/university						
Payments Variable $						
Groceries/meat/ vegetables						
Clothing/shoes						
Cars — service/ tyres/petrol						
Fares — train/bus						
Chemist/Dentist/ Doctor/Optometrist						

(continued)

	June	July	August	Sept	Oct	Nov	Dec	Total

	Jan	Feb	March	April	May
Newspapers/magazines/ books					
Home — painting/repairs/ garden					
Appliances/furniture — new/repairs					
Total Variable Payments					
Payments Discretionary $					
Holidays					
Entertainment — restaurants/movies					
Cigarettes/alcohol/ work lunch/takeaway					
Sports/hobbies/ club fees					
Children's pocket money/ toys					
Hair care/ dry-cleaning					
Gifts — Xmas/ birthday					
Donations					
Other					
Sundry cash — self					
Sundry cash — partner					
Surplus after expenses					

	June	July	August	Sept	Oct	Nov	Dec	Total

Money-saving tips

① Never pay retail

Everything's negotiable – you'll be surprised who will give you a discount, you just have to ask.

② Try in-house or plain-pack products

Buy the in-house brands – they almost always cost less than other brands but are usually of a similar quality.

③ Buy on special and use coupons

What can you buy on sale? Clothing in particular is well discounted halfway through and at the end of the season. Don't use this as an excuse, though, to purchase more than you need.

④ Plan your meals in advance and always use a pre-written shopping list

This will reduce the amount of items you buy that you really don't need. Try to do most of your shopping in one go instead of going to the corner store or supermarket regularly which is usually more expensive.

⑤ Buy used

New is nice, but for the best buy, think pre-owned or pre-loved. You will be amazed at what people don't want any more.

⑥ Pay cash

When you spend cash, it hurts and you tend to spend less. There have been studies done in the US which show that people spend considerably less when they pay cash than when they use a credit card.

⑦ Use family and community resources

This is something that a lot of new parents discover when faced with the cost of expensive baby goods that their child will soon outgrow. Rather than going out and buying a new cot, someone may have one you can borrow or buy from them. This can also be the same with furniture, appliances, electronic goods and clothing. Often we are in situations where we spent money on something we wanted, but it's outgrown its usefulness and someone else could have a use for it.

⑧ Hold the 'Mother of all Garage Sales'

Cast a critical eye over the stuff way at the back of your closets. If you haven't used it in six months, chances are you can do without it. Same goes for all that junk in storage. The website *www.trademe.co.nz* can be useful for both selling and buying used items.

⑨ Shop around for large-value items

It's often surprising how much the same item varies in price from store to store. Websites such as *www.applianceshopper.co.nz* will help you find the best price for big-ticket items.

⑩ Quit smoking

You may not be impressed by this option but it's incredible how much smoking will cost you over your lifetime – and that's not to mention what it saves you on insurance and healthcare.

⑪ Cut up and cancel your credit cards

Do you really need more than one credit card?

⑫ Save electricity

Turn off any unused appliances or electrical equipment. The electricity companies usually have brochures that offer a number of suggestions on ways to save on your power bill. The website *www.consumer.org.nz/powerswitch* also has some great hints on saving power.

⑬ Buy gifts on sale

Buy your gifts throughout the year when you see them on sale.

> ***Tip***
>
> 90% of solving a problem is recognising that you have one.

⑭ Beware of great deals that aren't that great

These may include:

- ◇ Interest-free
- ◇ Buy two for one
- ◇ No money now, pay in 12 months
- ◇ Warehouse stores that are more expensive than your regular shopping stores
- ◇ Loyalty cards that often encourage you to spend more to get the points.

⑮ Housing

This is the single biggest expense you face. Consider getting a flatmate or taking in a boarder. It may not be ideal but could provide some extra income for the short term.

⑯ Food

Take a packed lunch to work every day, and reduce the number of times you eat out and get takeaways. It also helps you keep to a healthy diet. Always use a shopping list.

⑰ Exercise restraint

Finally, call upon your willpower when it comes to spending. Want to save money on your phone bill? Hang up. Want to use less petrol? Stay home. Do you really need a breadmaker when you have an oven? Sometimes cutting costs really is just a matter of saying 'Enough is enough'.

Did you know?

A millionaire spends on average one minute longer on a mundane shopping transaction than a poor person. The extra time is taken for comparison shopping.

It's human nature to want something and want it now. Being willing to delay pleasure for a greater result is a sign of maturity. Developing a workable, realistic budget is without doubt one of the most important things you will do to help you achieve your goals. Household budgets, however, don't run themselves. When your budget breaks down, don't run away – take a deep breath, roll up your sleeves and get down to the hard work of knocking it back into shape.

There are only two things you can do
with money, save it or spend it.
If you spend it, it's gone forever!

In a nutshell

☆ Align your spending with your goals.

☆ Ask yourself do you really need it or do you simply just want it?

☆ Develop a manageable spending plan.

☆ Write down your plan and review it regularly.

☆ Establish an emergency fund.

6

Your biggest asset – your home

Be who you are and say what you feel, because those that mind don't matter and those who matter don't mind.

Dr Seuss

The difference between the ordinary and the extraordinary is that little bit extra.

Anon.

He who is afraid of doing too much always does too little.

German proverb

Never give up then, for that is just the place and time that the tide will turn.

Harriet Beecher Stowe

Buying vs renting

For most people their home is the most significant asset they will own in their lifetime. Not only does owning your home provide shelter, but also through mortgage repayments it provides a compulsory form of saving. In the last 20 years or so in New Zealand, homeownership has dropped from around 75% to close to 67%. Statistically speaking, that is quite a significant drop. The trend seems to indicate that the number of Kiwis owning their own home is continuing to decline.

Today we live in a more transient society. People move around a lot more with their jobs, are getting married later and want more flexibility with their living arrangements. There also doesn't seem to be as much emphasis placed on the importance of having your own home. Long-term renting is becoming more and more common. A concerning reason for this trend is that it's becoming increasingly difficult to afford to buy a home — firstly to save for the deposit, and secondly to be able to afford the mortgage repayments, especially in the major cities and more highly desirable and expensive areas. Housing affordability has increased from 60% of our income to 130% of our income over the last couple of decades. This basically means, looking at what we are earning today, it's more expensive for us to afford to buy a house than it was in our parents' generation.

In some cases you may be financially better off renting than buying your own home, providing you invest regularly so you accumulate a similar amount of money to what a freehold home would be worth, in say 20 years or so. The reality is, however, that most people don't have the discipline to do this and will therefore be better off buying a house and paying off the mortgage.

What are the main types of mortgages?

Principal & interest (P&I)

This is by far the most common type of mortgage and one that most homeowners will have. You pay interest and some principal in each mortgage repayment. At the end of the term of your loan you will have paid it off in full. In the first few years you will pay mainly interest and a small amount of principal, but as you get closer to the end of the loan, the amount of interest decreases and the amount of principal increases. This is because you pay interest on the outstanding balance, so as your loan balance decreases the less interest you pay and more of your repayments can be allocated to the principal.

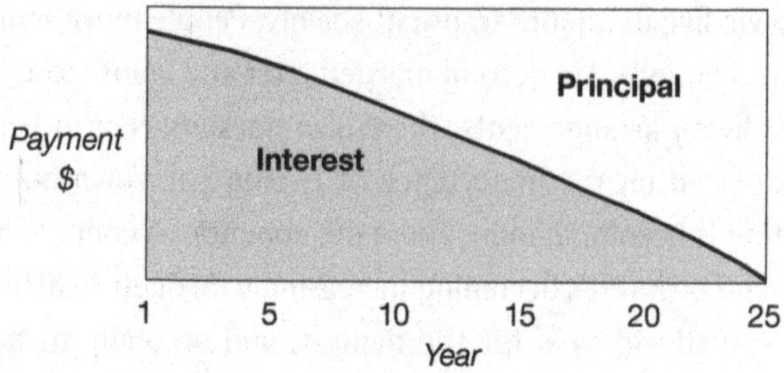

Interest only

With an interest-only loan you only pay the interest and no principal. At the end of the term of your loan you still owe the total amount of it. These loans are mainly for investment and business purposes and should not be used for your own home.

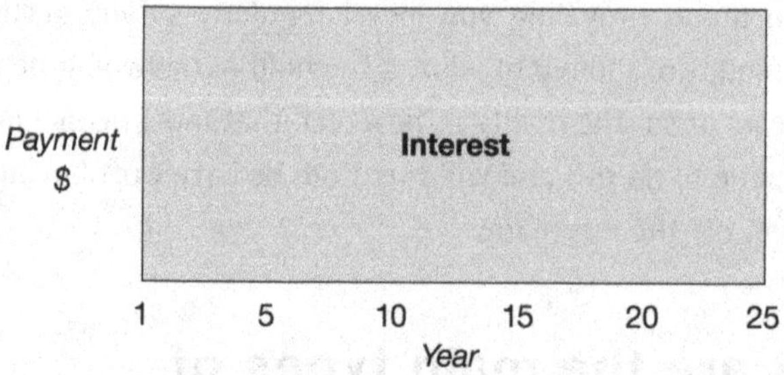

Revolving credit

There are a number of variations of revolving-credit mortgages. They give you the structure of a regular principal repayment schedule with the flexibility to repay as much as you like, and redraw the additional amounts paid should you wish. You can pay off as much as you like or simply pay the interest each month and you can re-borrow up to your limit any time you like, giving you ongoing access to credit. Since interest is calculated daily and charged monthly, the lower your average daily loan balance is, the less interest you are charged. These types of mortgages offer the greatest amount of flexibility; however, they can also be the most dangerous if you are not disciplined.

Floating/variable

A floating or variable mortgage is one where the interest rate on the loan goes up or down depending on what the market is doing. This means your repayments will increase or decrease if your lender changes their floating rates, i.e. if interest rates go up your repayments go up, if interest rates go down your repayments go down. This can make it more difficult to budget for your mortgage costs. These mortgages are more flexible though if you want to increase your regular payments or pay off lump sums.

Fixed

With a fixed mortgage the interest rate is set for a specific timeframe, usually from six months to three years. Some lenders do offer a five-year fixed rate. The advantage of a fixed rate is that you know exactly what your repayments will be for the timeframe you have fixed. The downside is that once they are set up you can not increase your regular payments. You can make a lump sum payment, but usually you can only do this once per year and there is a fee charged for doing so.

Did you know?

Housing affordability has increased from 60% to 130% of our income over the last couple of decades.

So what type of mortgage should you have?

There are a number of options available for you, and each bank or lending company has their own variation around the main types of mortgages. You need to look at what your requirements are before deciding on the best way to structure your mortgage. Fixing all of your mortgage on the cheapest rate might not be the best option for you as it makes it difficult to pay off the mortgage faster. However, if you can only afford the minimum payments and want to know exactly how much you need to pay each month, then it may be a good option.

If you want to pay your mortgage off faster, you may want to fix part of the mortgage and leave a small portion on revolving credit or variable terms. If you have a variable income, revolving credit mortgages can be an excellent way for you to manage your payments. You can use your revolving credit facility as your emergency fund (as discussed in the previous chapter). But if you are not very disciplined with money, it is best to stay away from revolving credit mortgages.

Fixed vs floating rates

Whether it is cheaper to fix or float your mortgage is a commonly asked question. Some years it will be cheaper (i.e. due to a lower interest rate) to fix your mortgage, in other years it will be cheaper to have a floating rate. This is because the market rates for mortgages change when the Official Cash Rate (OCR) changes. The OCR is one of the mechanisms used by the Reserve Bank (on behalf of the government) to control monetary policy in New Zealand. Over the length of a mortgage it is likely that your interest costs will be similar if you either mainly fix or

> ***Did you know?***
>
> Homeownership in NZ has decreased from 75% to almost 67% and is continuing to drop.

float – i.e. your interest costs will average out. The main advantage of fixing is that you know exactly how much your payments are each month, while the main advantage of floating is more flexibility. So it really comes down to what type of mortgage suits your individual needs.

Mortgage insurance

If you borrow more than 80% of the value of your home you will probably have to pay mortgage insurance. This insures the bank in case you are unable to repay your loan. It doesn't, however, insure you and your payments. It is usually a one-off payment when you take the mortgage out. The rate varies but it is approximately 0.5 to 1% of the total value of the loan. If you take out a $100,000 mortgage, mortgage insurance will cost you $500–$1000 depending on the lender you use.

Using an independent mortgage broker

I am a big fan of using a professional mortgage broker. The problem with going to a bank or finance company yourself is that you are only dealing with the lending products which that particular company offers. A mortgage broker, on the other hand, has access to and knowledge about all the products available in the market and can find the one that best suits your individual needs. They can also be extremely good at negotiating reduced loan application fees and getting you a contribution towards your legal costs and valuation fees.

Mortgage register

In my experience, most people aren't really sure what type of mortgage they have. You can use the register on the next page to write down what you currently have so that you have a record of your mortgage. A suggestion would be to go to your bank or mortgage broker and review whether your mortgage structure is still suitable for your needs. You may want to do this every few years or when your fixed rate falls due or if your circumstances change.

Mortgage Company	Fixed/Floating/ Revolving Credit	Amount of Loan	Interest Rate	Term (i.e. 25 years)	Fortnightly or Monthly Amount	Annual Mortgage Interest Cost
Total		$			$	$

Save thousands of dollars

Accelerating your mortgage payments will guarantee that you can save thousands of dollars over the term of a normal 25-year loan. In other words, making extra payments on your mortgage is one of the most effective ways to save money. However, most people don't realise the significance of small additional payments over a period of time.

One thing I always do with clients who have a mortgage is work out if they can afford to pay if off more quickly. In general, I find that people tend to pay their mortgages off on the standard 25-year term. Probably because firstly they get into the habit of it, and secondly because they have no idea of how much interest they will save by fast-tracking their payments. Once we complete an exercise showing how much can be saved by increasing their regular payments each month, not only are they astounded by the amounts, but they suddenly develop a strong motivation to pay off their mortgage much faster.

Most bank and mortgage-broking websites have simple calculators that you can use to work out how much your mortgage is costing you. I have done some calculations in the table below to give you an idea:

$100,000	**25 years**	**20 years**	**15 years**	**10 years**
Interest rate	7.5%	7.5%	7.5%	7.5%
Monthly payment	$739	$806	$927	$1187
Total interest paid	$121,697	$93,341	$66,861	$42,442
$150,000	**25 years**	**20 years**	**15 years**	**10 years**
Interest rate	7.5%	7.5%	7.5%	7.5%
Monthly payment	$1108	$1280	$1390	$1780
Total interest paid	$182,547	$140,013	$100,293	$63,663
$200,000	**25 years**	**20 years**	**15 years**	**10 years**
Interest rate	7.5%	7.5%	7.5%	7.5%
Monthly payment	$1477	$1611	$1854	$2374
Total interest paid	$243,394	$186,685	$133,723	$84,884

Tom and Sonya, a young couple in their late 20s, both had good jobs and between them were earning around $100,000 per year, plus Tom earned a small bonus. They had recently purchased their own home in Auckland with a 90% mortgage of $300,000. They were keen to start investing and had heard a lot about property as a good investment option. They wanted to know how to get started. During our meeting I discovered that they were paying their mortgage off over the standard 25-year term even though they could afford a lot more. We discussed how they could manage their income and spending more effectively so they could work towards paying off their mortgage in 10 years, as apposed to the 25-year payment plan they were on. Using an interest rate of 7.5% their monthly payments went from $2216 p/m to $3561 p/m and they would save approximately $229,000 in interest by paying off the mortgage 15 years earlier. I doubt whether they would have made anywhere near that amount of money from a rental property in 10 years.

Should you pay off your mortgage before investing?

From a purely financial perspective you are usually better off paying your mortgage off before you start a savings or investment programme. This is because you pay your mortgage with money you earn after tax. Therefore, to be better off financially by investing you need to earn a return of approximately 10–11% gross per annum (about 7–8% after tax). There are not many investments that will produce this level of return unless you take on a reasonable amount of risk.

However, the reality is that we are dealing with human psychology. This means that because we are dealing with emotion, desire, discipline and so on people rarely do anything for purely financial reasons. I typically find that people will pay off their mortgages in the same timeframe regardless of whether they are putting money aside for investment or not. Usually I would recommend, if you can afford it, paying off your mortgage faster than the standard 25-year term, and also contributing to a regular savings or investment plan. One of the positives about starting an investment plan while you still have a mortgage is that you start to get into the habit of savings, which is a great discipline to have to help you achieve your financial goals. Remember, you still need to have an emergency fund equivalent to 3–6 months of your expenses.

Finally . . .

Beware of getting into the trap of continually upgrading your home. I have seen people who have spent their entire working lives trying to get on top of their mortgage payments because they keep buying bigger and more expensive homes. When they get to retirement, the only asset they have is a beautiful home but almost no money to live on. This is known as being asset rich but cash poor. The reality is that cash flow is king. It's your cash flow that provides money for you to live on.

I would strongly encourage you to fast-track your mortgage payments. Once you have a freehold home, not only will you have a sense of freedom and accomplishment, you will also have so much more disposable income to do the things you dream about.

In a nutshell

- ☆ Buying your home is a great way of compulsory saving.
- ☆ Put some thought into the best type of mortgage for your needs as opposed to fixing it at the cheapest rate.
- ☆ Pay your mortgage off as fast as you can.

7

Beware the great trap: Debt

Bad habits are like a comfortable bed,
easy to get into, but hard to get out of.

Anon.

Failure is only the opportunity to begin again,
more intelligently.

Henry Ford

Continuing to do the same thing over and
over again and expecting a different result
is the definition of insanity.

Albert Einstein

Debt is not a tool

A major barrier to gaining control of your finances is your view of debt. Debt is becoming increasingly ingrained in our culture. Those who are comfortable with consumer debt will always struggle to get their personal finances under control. However, debt is not a tool – it's a method to make banks and finance companies wealthy. I have a very strong view on consumer debt, and that is *avoid it like the plague*. It may be a harsh viewpoint; however, most of the people I know who are good money-managers and are in a good financial position share this outlook.

Credit-card debt quadruples

Early in 2005, the total credit-card debt in New Zealand was nudging $4 billion, having been only $1 billion five years before. That is a pretty frightening statistic. We now live in a cashless society where it is so easy to put everything on credit. Many people get to the end of the month and have no idea what they have put on credit throughout that month.

The problem is that many people don't have the discipline to manage their credit cards effectively. Recent surveys suggest that only half of credit-card holders pay off their balance in full each month. Credit-card companies on average charge close to 20% interest on the amount outstanding, and in 2004 we were charged around $500 million in total interest.

Mindlessly following others

Just because other people are doing it doesn't mean it's a smart thing to do. Sometimes we don't realise that what we are doing is stupid, either because it's the way we perceive it has always been done or because other people are doing it too. We don't ask why, we just follow.

A book I read recently (*Competing for the Future* by Gary Hamel and C.K. Prahalad) illustrates the point well. It was about a study done on monkeys:

A group of monkeys were locked in a room with a pole in the middle. Some luscious, ripe bananas were put at the top of the pole. When a monkey began to climb the pole, the researchers would knock it off with a blast of water from a fire hose. Each time a monkey would climb, they would be knocked off, thus learning that the climb was hopeless. The researchers then observed that, after a while, when a monkey would begin to climb, the other monkeys would pull down the monkey trying to climb. They replaced a single monkey with one that did not know the system. Sure enough, as soon as the new monkey began to climb the others pulled him down and punished him for trying. One by one all the monkeys were replaced so that none of the monkeys had experienced the fire hose. Yet each time a new monkey tried to climb the pole the others pulled him down. None of the monkeys knew why they weren't allowed to climb the pole to get the bananas. It was just the way it was.

The lesson: Just because other people think that consumer debt is okay, it doesn't mean you should.

What is consumer debt?

Consumer debt is all debt except for your mortgage on your own home or investment debt (i.e. debt on an asset that makes you money). Just to clarify, cars are not an investment. I have had a few clients over the years try to justify their car purchase as an investment, but unless you are in the business of buying and selling cars, you are out of luck: it's not an investment! The different types of debt are shown in the table opposite.

> ***Did you know?***
> In 2004, New Zealanders paid over $490 million in credit-card interest.

Type	Lender	Purpose	Fees	Interest Rates
Personal loan	Bank	Car, home improvements, holidays	Usually 1%	15–20% depending on the bank and what security is offered
Overdraft	Bank	Ongoing expenses	Set-up fee plus an ongoing monthly fee	15–20% depending on the bank and what security is offered
Credit cards	Bank	Anything, providing you stay under your limit	$20 to a few hundred dollars, depending on benefits offered, i.e. air points	13–21% (most are around 20%)
Hire Purchase	Retail outlets	Consumer items	Set-up fee, some have no charges, insurance is sometimes required	Usually around 20%
Home loan	Bank, Finance companies	Property	Varies, usually a loan application fee	6.5–8% Banks 8%+ Finance companies
Student loan	Government	Tertiary education	$50	Approx. 7%
Loan	Bank, Finance companies	Varies	Varies	Varies depending on the lender and what security is offered

How much do you owe?

How wonderful it would be to hear the word *nothing* when I ask this question. Unfortunately, that is not the reality for many people. Before you work out a plan for getting rid of your debt, you need to establish exactly what you owe. Interestingly, many people don't actually know this – I guess because it's pretty scary and they think they are better off not knowing! Complete the table opposite and work out what your position is.

Slaying the plastic monster

While it can be discouraging to face a mountain of credit-card and consumer debt, it's important to remember that there is a way out. The key is to systematically confront your debt with sound tactics designed to accelerate your repayments and reduce the overall interest you pay.

① Stop charging!

If you can't afford to buy something without using a credit card or hire purchase, do without. While this may feel a bit painful at first, many people find that the things they've been buying with credit are things they don't really need.

② Double (or triple or quadruple) your payments on the credit card with the highest interest

This card is costing you the most, so concentrate on paying it off first. Once it's taken care of, move on to the card with the next-highest interest.

Did you know?

47% of the 18–24-year-olds and 31% of the 25–34-year-olds have negative wealth (where debts exceed assets).

Consumer debt register

Type of Debt	Interest Rate	Total Owed	Monthly Payment	Annual Payment	Total Interest Cost
Credit cards					
Store cards (e.g. Farmers card)					
Hire Purchases					
Car loans					
Family loans					
Student loan					
Other					
TOTAL		$	$	$	$

Did you know?

Is it really 'interest free'? Try asking for the cash price. The discount is the hidden interest you were about to pay.

③ Use your 'extra' money

Whenever you receive additional income from a tax refund, gift, pay rise, and so on, commit it to debt repayment. Since you hadn't planned on this income, you won't miss it. Those extra payments do make a big difference.

④ Dig into savings

If you have some money stashed away in a low-interest account (like a savings account), think about using it to pay off some debt. Your savings account is only paying you a very small interest rate, but you're paying much more than that on your debt.

⑤ Keep going

By the time you've paid off your credit-card debt, you'll have developed a great set of money-management skills. Put them to work on an investment programme that will put your money to work to fund your long-term dreams.

Do you really need a credit card?

Credit cards can be incredibly convenient. They can also be one of your biggest problems when it comes to gaining control of your spending. It's just too darn easy to use them. Be honest with yourself, do you really need a credit card? I agree that credit cards are extremely useful, but do you *really* need them? Are they far too dangerous in your hands?

Many people have a number of credit cards. If you have one for business and one for personal that's a little different but there are few reasons why you need more than one. Ask yourself if you really need it;

if *No,* take the scissors to it and then cancel it. If you decide *Yes* and find it a little difficult to manage your spending:

- ◇ read the conditions carefully to make sure that the type of card suits your needs;
- ◇ set a credit-card limit that suits your budget;
- ◇ know what the interest rate is;
- ◇ pay off the balance every month (then you won't be paying any interest); and
- ◇ make sure you know exactly how much you are putting on your card every month and that it fits into your budget.

If you are still struggling – *don't take it shopping with you (you can always go back if it's important) or lock it away and only use it for emergencies.*

Note: *Credit cards are okay, if you pay them off in full every month, and also if you don't get into bad habits because you aren't handing over the cash and aren't aware of exactly what you are spending.*

Should you consolidate your debts?

Putting all your debts into one personal loan can be a good option for some people. Personal loans generally have a lower interest rate than the rate you pay on your credit cards. They also have very strict repayment plans, whereas on your credit cards you decide on your repayments.

> ***Did you know?***
>
> On average, a new car loses 60% of its value in the first four years. It's better to be the second owner.

However, I have mixed views on whether this approach works or not. It can definitely save you money due to the lower interest rate you pay, but in my experience it just moves the issue sideways for many people. They consolidate all their debts into one personal loan, but then go and put more money on their credit cards.

If you are going to consolidate your loans you need to be totally committed to paying off your debts. You could cut up and cancel your credit card until your debts are paid. It's easy – probably too easy – to get another card when you have your finances under control. A less drastic option may be to give your card to a close friend or family member for *safekeeping* under strict instructions that they give it back to you only in the case of an emergency or when you have paid off your debts.

Student loans

The increasing amount of student debt in New Zealand is very concerning and has been subject to a lot of political debate. I am not going to go into this area in detail. However, I will say that if you are currently a student or you have children who are students, you need to make certain that student loans are being used for course costs and living costs, not discretionary spending. I am amazed at how many students I see who eat out regularly, drive nice cars, wear expensive clothes, travel, and so on. I think one of the big reasons for this is that they really don't understand how the debt adds up, how compounding interest affects the amount of the debt once they finish their courses, and the effect it has down the track on their ability to save for a house

> ***Did you know?***
>
> 413,000 New Zealanders have a student loan, with an average debt of about $14,400. Over 100,000 owe more than $20,000.

> **Tip**
>
> Be very wary of guaranteeing a loan for someone else, even if it's a family member.

or accumulate investment assets. If you do have a student debt, then you need to work on paying it off as soon as you can, just like any other debt.

Lisa Schulz wrote a very comprehensive book, *Get Rid of Your Student Loan Now*, solely about student debt (see Recommended Reading List, page 157). It is well worth reading for anyone with student debt.

So what about reward points?

These are a great bonus, but that's all they are. Companies have spent enormous amounts of money in recent years developing and running various loyalty schemes. Their sole focus is to get you to spend more money. Purchasing something that you don't necessarily need just to get reward points is, when you think about it, a total false economy. By that I mean you are effectively buying something to get a 1% or so discount towards a future purchase or gift. If you are already planning to buy an item, you have budgeted for it, *and* it so happens that you get reward points, then that's a great bonus. Every little bit adds up and these reward points can be a good way of saving you money – but only if you genuinely *need* the item and are not buying it just for the sake of a bit of retail therapy or accumulating points.

The bottom line!

There are two types of people: those who pay interest and those who save interest. Those that become interest savers as opposed to interest payers will always be far better off financially. Besides making you feel awful, debt is your main barrier to building a financially secure future.

Developing an *allergic reaction* to debt is one of the most effective ways to help you achieve a strong financial position. Learn to live by the philosophy of *if you can't pay cash for it, you can't afford to buy it.* I cannot stress strongly enough how important this is. *Forbes Magazine* did a survey of the 'Forbes 400' (a list of the 400 richest Americans): 75% of them said that the best way to build wealth is to become and stay debt free.

If you can't afford it
. . . don't buy it!

In a nutshell

☆ Don't put your head in the sand. Put together a plan for paying off your debts as soon as you can.

☆ If you can't afford it – don't buy it!

☆ If you can't afford it – don't buy it!

☆ If you can't afford it – don't buy it!

8

Planning for what might happen: Insurance

Obstacles are those frightful things you see
when you take your eyes off your goal.

Henry Ford

If you think insurance is expensive,
try paying the claim.

Anon.

Most of the important things in the world
have been accomplished by people who have kept
on trying when there seemed to be no hope at all.

Dale Carnegie

Have you ever met a widow who thought
her husband was overinsured?

Anon.

We all hate insurance – until we need it.

Anon.

Insurance — you can't afford not to have it

Insurance is a necessary evil. Unfortunately, it is not something you can go out and buy when you need it. Insurance is about planning for the 'what ifs' in life before they happen.

The basis of insurance is the insured passes risks which they are unable to or are not prepared to fund if an event arises and it provides dollars when you can't.

The most common excuse when it comes to not having insurance is that 'I can't afford it'. The reality is that in most cases you can not afford *not* to have it. Most people, unless well advised, buy the wrong insurance. I often find people are overinsured in one area and underinsured in another. The key thing is to work out what risks you face. Ideally, it would be best to do this with a qualified risk broker who can help you determine what risks you wish to transfer (insure) and which you are comfortable self-insuring (i.e. you will live with the consequences).

General insurance

House insurance

There are two types of house insurance:

Insured value: This pays a specific amount based on the market value of your home at the time you take out the policy. It is the cheapest option but is not often used as it often doesn't cover the amount needed if you had to rebuild your property or take into account any increases in your property value.

Replacement cover: This is worked out on the square metre size of your property (the building/improvements) and will cover the cost of rebuilding your property regardless of the cost. This is the cover most people use.

Contents insurance

This covers the contents of your house and other belongings while they are in your house or if they are elsewhere temporarily. In the event of loss some items are paid out at their replacement value (cost to replace), while others are paid out at their indemnity value (i.e. market value if they were sold). If you have expensive items like a camera or jewellery, you may want to itemise them on your policy.

Car insurance

Car insurance will cover the cost of any damage you cause to your own car or someone else's car. There are two main types:

Third-party cover: This is the most basic insurance, and is therefore the cheapest. It covers you for causing damage to someone else's car.

Comprehensive cover: This covers any damage caused by you to your car or to another person's car.

Personal insurance

What are the types of risks you could encounter? You need to consider the financial strain you and your family could face in a number of situations. Below I have outlined the main types of personal insurance. As people often struggle to understand the situations in which they may need insurance cover, I have included examples below of each type of insurance.

Life insurance

Life insurance provides a lump sum payable when the policy owner dies. It could be used to eliminate any debts, pay off the mortgage, cover funeral costs, pay for the future education of children and provide an income for the spouse and family. There are two main types:

Endowment and Whole of Life policies. These have higher premiums because they have a savings component to them. I am not a big fan of these policies because insurance and investment are quite different and I don't believe they work well combined in the same product.

Term Life policies. This is simply a set amount of cover for a set time period. These policies are cheaper than endowment policies because there is no investment component to them.

Whole of Life policies are often referred to as bundled policies and Term Life policies are known as unbundled policies.

Geraldine and Simon and their three young children were living a comfortable life. They had a lovely house in the country, Simon had a great job with a good salary and Geraldine ran a part-time business from home. One day, at the young age of 43, Simon had a sudden heart attack and died. They had life cover in place but unfortunately it was only enough to just cover the mortgage. Geraldine, faced with her own grief and looking after three small children who had just lost their father, was finding life a real struggle. Unfortunately, unless she got the business running again they would have no money to live on. Geraldine now regretted not taking the advice of their risk broker and increasing Simon's life insurance cover.

Income protection

Also known as disability income, this is one of the most important types of insurance. It gives you the ability to insure one of your most valuable assets: your ability to earn an income. For example, if you earn $50,000 per annum and are now aged 40, your future income is $1.25 million (25 years x $50,000). It is the potential loss of this income that an income protection policy insures against. A monthly income is paid to you if you are not able to work due to an illness or injury. Your policy will have a waiting period of four, eight or 13 weeks, chosen by you, before any income is paid. You are able to insure up to 75% of your taxable income under most income protection policies. Let me stress this again – your ability to earn an income is one of the most valuable assets you have.

At 47, Claire had it all – a high-powered career as a human resources consultant and a young child she adored. However, Claire realised that as the sole income provider she and her daughter needed some security in case she was unable to work. Just two years later, a mammogram revealed that Claire had cancer. Through her income protection policy she received a benefit of $3200 a month. This benefit provided Claire with financial help so she could stop worrying about money and concentrate on getting well.

Total and permanent disablement

If you suffer a permanent disability, this type of insurance may pay you a lump sum. There is usually a minimum six-month period before the payment is made so the disability can be verified as permanent. This type of insurance is usually inexpensive.

Simon and Jane found that they got to the end of each month with just enough money to live on. Their two children were at school so Jane was able to work and provide a much-needed supplementary income. They had sought advice from an insurance broker and agreed they needed a full protection plan. However, they only took out a life insurance policy as it was not only the cheapest but it was where they thought their greatest risk was. Unfortunately Simon became ill, was confined to bed and unable to work. Simon's company kindly paid his wages for a couple of weeks but that was all they could afford and they had to let him go. Six months later Simon wasn't improving and was still confined to bed most of the day. Simon may have been entitled to get a lump sum from a total and permanent disablement policy had he taken out the policy his advisor had recommended to him.

Did you know?

On average we each have a one in eight chance of having a stroke in our lifetime.

Stroke Foundation of New Zealand, 2004

About 80% of all cancers are thought to be related to lifestyle and environmental factors.

Cancer Society of New Zealand, 2003

One in seven New Zealanders will die during their working lives.

Demographic Trends, *Statistics New Zealand, 2001*

In 2000, the major cause of death was cancer followed by ischaemic heart disease.

Mortality and Demographic Data, *New Zealand Health Service, 2000*

There were 7620 deaths caused by cancer in 2000 with males making up 54% of all cases.

Cancer Registrations, *New Zealand Health Service, 2000*

There were 85 ACC claims for fatal injury in 2001–02 with only four of these cases for females. Males aged 65 and over had the highest incidence rate.

Injury Statistics, Work-Related Claims, *Statistics New Zealand, 2003*

Trauma protection

Sometimes referred to as serious illness cover, this cover will provide a lump sum payment, payable if you suffer a trauma or critical illness, such as a heart attack, stroke or cancer. This type of trauma may result in many unforeseen expenses such as the cost of medical treatment, rehabilitation (including career retraining) and home help.

At 57 John had a great life. He had spent 15 years building up his very successful consultancy business. With his two children now grown up and independent, John and his wife were enjoying the freedom to pack up and go sailing whenever they wished.

Then John suffered a heart attack, which immediately confined him to bed and kept him off work — and the boat — for three months. Through his trauma protection cover, John was paid a lump sum of $50,500. He also received income protection payments of $3922 and a bed confinement payment of $227. With no financial stress, John could concentrate on getting well, and three months later he was back in business.

Medical insurance

With the constantly rising cost of medical care and hospital waiting lists growing all the time, this insurance enables you to receive private medical care quickly. There are two main types of medical insurance: basic policies cover you for hospitalisation and specialist care, and comprehensive policies will also cover visits to the doctor and dentist.

Derrick, at 58, was a married father of three with a hectic lifestyle juggling family commitments and work as a store manager. When he suffered a heart attack everything changed. Not only did Derrick have to slow down, but he really needed angioplasty — a procedure that would reopen his blocked blood vessels. He could wait for public treatment, or get it done privately — at a cost of $11,473. With his medical insurance policy he was able to have the procedure done almost immediately at a private hospital.

Did you know?

The leading causes of death between the ages of 15–24 were from external causes such as accidents, violence and poisoning.

NZ Age Specific Death Rates 2000–2002, *Statistics New Zealand, 2002*

30–40% of all amputations are performed on patients with diabetes.

www.vascular.co.nz, 2004

The leading cause of disability is disease or illness (40%), followed by accident or injury (30%).

Statistics New Zealand

Three-quarters of all claims for work-related injuries in 2003 were made by males.

Injury Statistics, Work-Related Claims, *ACC New Zealand, 2003*

More injuries affected the hand and wrist than any other bodily location in 2003.

Injury Statistics, Main Findings, *ACC New Zealand, 2003*

Workers aged between 25 and 54 accounted for 69% of all work-related injuries.

Injury Statistics, Main Findings, *ACC New Zealand, 2003*

A 35-year-old has a one in five chance of suffering a critical illness before age 65.

Davies Financial and Actuarial

What insurance do you currently have?

It's important to establish firstly what insurance cover you currently have, so complete the chart on pages 108–109.

How do you know if you have enough insurance?

You need to consider the financial strain you and your family may confront if you are unable to work for an extended period. By an extended period I mean 3–6 months or possibly longer. Hopefully you will have an emergency fund set aside so you can cover your living costs for that period. After that you need to ask yourself if you will be able to maintain your current lifestyle and still afford:

- ◇ day-to-day living expenses
- ◇ insurance premiums such as house, contents or life cover
- ◇ hire purchase and credit-card payments
- ◇ a planned holiday
- ◇ mortgage repayments
- ◇ existing debts
- ◇ business debts and running costs
- ◇ counselling, rehabilitation or career retraining costs
- ◇ medical expenses
- ◇ childcare
- ◇ children's school fees both now and in the future
- ◇ retirement funding
- ◇ continued management of your business.

Insurances	Policy No.	Company/Agent	
Fire & General			
House	....	....	
Contents	....	....	
Car	....	....	
Boat	....	....	
Motorbike	....	....	
Health			
Comprehensive	....	....	
Hospital/specialist only	....	....	
Life			
Trauma			
Total Permanent Disability			
Disability Income			
Business			
Key person	....	....	
Business overheads	....	....	
Professional indemnity	....	....	
Public liability	....	....	
Loss of profits	....	....	
Business pack	....	....	

	Amount of Cover	Monthly Premium	Annual Premium
	Total Premiums	**$**	**$**

Susan and Tom are a happily married couple in their 30s. Tom works to support the family and earns an income before tax of $70,000 pa. Susan is at home looking after the children and running the household. Consider the following:

1. Tom becomes disabled through sickness or an accident and is unable to work for 12 months. ACC would possibly pay 80% of Tom's income if it was an accident, but not if it was due to illness (as in 75% of cases). If Tom is disabled, how would the mortgage and day-to-day living costs be paid?
2. Tom is totally disabled and is unable to ever return to the workforce. Could Susan go out to work and earn a similar income and become the financial provider for the family? Who would look after Tom and the children?
3. Susan dies suddenly. Could Tom still work and look after the children or would he have to pay for full-time childcare? How much would this cost and could he afford it?
4. Tom dies suddenly. How would Susan pay the living costs and continue to pay the extra expenses on their rental properties? Would she have to go back into the workforce? Can she earn a similar income? Who would look after the children or how would childcare be afforded?

These are some of the risks that need to be considered when looking at an insurance plan for yourself or your family. None of us like insurance but it is an important part of our lives. Generally we are pretty comfortable insuring our property, car and household contents but when it comes to insuring ourselves we are more reluctant.

The following example will help Tom and Susan work out how much life cover they may need:

Calculating the amount of life cover you need

Calculating insurance cover needs on the death of	Tom	Susan
Cash Needs: **(to pay immediate expenses)**		
Final expenses (funeral, legal, medical)	$25,000	$25,000
Superannuation funding	0	0
Repay mortgages, hire purchase, etc	$220,000	$220,000
Education fund	$50,000	$50,000
Liquidity for 12 months	$50,000	$50,000
Total cash needs:	**$345,000**	**$345,000**
Income Needs: **(to provide income for dependants)**		
Annual family income in the event of your death (including provision for home help for children)	$40,000	$30,000
How many years you wish to provide this for	10	10
Total capital required to meet income needs:	**$400,000**	**$300,000**
Less Funds Available:		
Existing life insurances	0	0
Superannuation benefits	$50,000	0
Saleable asset	0	0
Other available funds	0	0
Total funds available:	**$50,000**	**0**
LIFE COVER NEEDS	**$745,000**	**$645,000**
Shortfall	**$695,000**	**$645,000**

Notes:
This table only takes into account life cover requirements and is solely an indication of how a situation is looked at when developing a risk plan; each family or business has its own set of risks and should be looked at and assessed individually.

With the example above, income protection, and trauma and permanent disability cover would be recommended for Tom, as well as a family medical policy. You may be thinking this amount of cover is likely to be expensive. But the important thing is to understand your risks, how much you are happy to self-insure (i.e. not have an insurance policy to cover), and then take out the appropriate insurance policies you need to cover the risks you are not comfortable with. I can not stress enough how important it is to get professional advice in this area, and that you must review your requirements regularly.

8 tips for saving money on your insurance

① Increase the level of your excess.

② Obtain a discount by installing smoke and burglar alarms.

③ Obtain a discount by having all of your insurances with one company.

④ Pay your insurance annually. There is a premium of approximately 9% on your insurance if you pay monthly.

⑤ Be careful when making a claim. Ensure that what you get paid out is worth more than the cost of losing your no-claims bonus.

⑥ Shop around – some companies offer discounts for different social or age groups.

⑦ Extend the waiting period on your income protection. (Note that you need to ensure you have an emergency fund in place or available funds to cover you for this extended period.)

⑧ Review your insurances regularly to make sure you have enough cover and to ensure that you are not overinsured. As a general rule of thumb, as your net worth increases the need for life insurance decreases.

In a nutshell

☆ Insurance is about planning for the 'what ifs' in life.

☆ Think about the risks you and your family face – are you willing to take on those risks yourself or should you pass them on to an insurance company?

☆ Get good professional advice to make sure you have the correct insurance for your individual situation and ensure you are not over- or under-insured.

☆ Review your policies regularly.

9

You can't take it with you

Grant me the serenity to accept the things that I cannot change;
The courage to change the things I can;
And the wisdom to know the difference.

Reinhold Niebuhr

Nobody hands you excellence on a silver platter.
You learn it through planning, preparing, and
persisting in the face of all obstacles.

Anon.

Sometimes the best place to find a helping hand
is at the end of your own arm.

Swedish proverb

He who dies with the most toys still dies.

Anon.

Planning your estate

The old saying goes that the two things in life that are inevitable are death and taxes. You can't do anything about death, but at some stage someone is going to have to look after your affairs. The aim of estate planning is to minimise emotional and financial hardship for the people you care about.

An up-to-date will is still the cornerstone of a good estate plan.

What is a will?

◇ A will gives instructions for the orderly distribution of your assets after you die.

◇ Your will names the beneficiaries (the people who will benefit) of your estate, and sets out which of your possessions and other property you want them to receive.

◇ A will is legally binding and its instructions come into effect when the person who has made the will dies.

◇ If you are a male making a will you are the testator, if you are a female you are the testatrix. Those who you want to give your property to are your beneficiaries; those who you want to look after your property and administer your estate once you have died are your executors and trustees.

◇ To make a valid will you must be of a sound mind and 18 years of age or over.

◇ You can alter and rewrite your will as many times as you like.

◇ It must be in writing, signed by the testator/testatrix and have two witnesses who are not beneficiaries.

Why do you need a will?

You never know what is going to happen tomorrow. If you plan responsibly for your future you will make it much easier for your family and loved ones when your life's journey finally comes to an end.

Your death may be one of the most stressful things in life that your loved ones have to face. A will can provide more certainty and comfort to you and to those who may deal with your estate as well as minimise the chances of discontent within your surviving family. If you have children you can appoint guardians for them and outline your provisions for them.

Why people generally don't have a will

In New Zealand a surprising number of people do not have a will. I have certainly found with the clients I have seen over the years that only a small percentage have a current will. Often those who do have a will haven't updated it in years. Some of the common reasons are:

- ◊ I'm too young
- ◊ My family already know my wishes
- ◊ I don't own enough to give anything away
- ◊ I don't have kids yet
- ◊ I'm single and don't have a partner or children
- ◊ I'm married and my partner and I own half each
- ◊ Wills are too expensive to make
- ◊ I'm too busy, there's plenty of time
- ◊ I don't want to think about dying.

What happens if you die without a will?

If you don't have a will, you die intestate and your wishes may not be carried out. It can take a long time and a lot of money to sort out your estate. After any debts and costs are paid, your estate is divided amongst your relatives.

This is what can happen if you don't have a will

Are you married?

Yes	No
Your partner gets some, your children get the rest.	Everything goes to the children.
↓	↓
No children Your partner and parents share.	**No children** It all goes to your parents.
↓	↓
Parents dead It all goes to your partner.	**Parents dead** Certain blood relatives get it.
	↓
	No relatives Everything goes to the government.

If I have a will when should it be updated?

Generally it should be reviewed approximately every three years or upon a significant change in your circumstances such as:

- ◊ Marriage or remarriage
- ◊ Separation, divorce, starting a de facto relationship
- ◊ Birth of children or grandchildren
- ◊ Special needs of dependants
- ◊ When setting up a family trust
- ◊ Acquisition or disposal of a major asset
- ◊ Death of a loved one

Where do I go to get a will?

You can either have a will set up by your lawyer or a public trustee company like the Public Trust or Guardian Trust. I would be cautious using one of the DIY will kits that are available on the market – I am not convinced they are particularly effective as you don't actually receive any advice.

Katherine left this world in her late 80s after leading a healthy life almost to the end. Although she had an up-to-date will it wasn't overly specific. She had provided instructions on how her property was to be distributed but had failed to mention anything about her funeral or where she was to be buried. She had said before she passed away that she didn't want a funeral. Of course, the family thought that they needed to have one but a heated discussion followed about how the funeral would be run. She wasn't religious at all but some of the family thought the funeral should be in a church, while other family members thought that she wouldn't want it to be in a church. Once a decision was made another discussion followed around whether she should be cremated or buried, the family differing in their opinions once again. To top it all off, the family could not agree where she should be buried – with her husband (who she didn't like very much in the later stages of their marriage) or next to her family. A decision couldn't be reached and she ended up in a jar on a mantelpiece in a family member's home. Although these seem fairly simple issues, at such an emotional time, they create an enormous amount of stress and can cause major problems within a family.

Will checklist

The following two pages contain a checklist that you can use to assemble the information you will need in order to complete your will.

Personal Information

Full name

Date of birth

Place of birth

Current occupation

Marital/relationship status

If in a de facto relationship, when did your relationship commence?

Information about your spouse or partner

Full name (including any other names they may be known by)

Date of birth

Current occupation

Information about your children

(including adopted children)

Full names of your children

Date of birth of your children

Intended beneficiaries

Full names of all intended beneficiaries

Date of birth of all intended beneficiaries

Executors and trustees

(ideally at least two)

Full names

Current occupations

Will you require a professional person or trustee company to be a trustee? If so, have you considered their fee?

Guardians

(if appropriate)

Full names

Current occupations

Information about your estate

Bank account details

Life insurance policies

Debts owed to you

Investments

Real estate

Home contents and furnishings

Personal chattels

Motor vehicles

Boats

Any mortgages

Other monies you owe

Guarantees you have in place

Disposal of remains and funeral directions

What kind of funeral do you want?

Do you want to donate any body organs for medical research?

Do you want to be buried or cremated, and are there any special requests related to that?

Disposal of personal effects

Specific gifts to spouse/partner, children and others

Furniture

Clothing

Jewellery

Valuable collections

Motor vehicles

Boats

How is the remainder of your personal effects to be divided among the beneficiaries?

Monetary gifts

Amount (in figures and words)

Name and/or details of the individual or organisation receiving the monetary gift

Enduring powers of attorney – anticipate the unexpected

There are many instances when not being able to manage your own affairs could have serious consequences for you or your family – and could also result in financial loss. It could be through ill health, as the result of an accident, or it may simply be that you are overseas on business or on holiday. An enduring power of attorney is an essential document in planning for your life. It is a legal document which operates during your lifetime and which appoints an attorney to act on your behalf when you can not.

If you become incapacitated you should have both enduring powers of attorney to provide for your personal care and welfare as well as the ongoing management of your assets and financial arrangements. Unlike a will, which is activated on death, powers of attorney only have relevance when you are alive.

Enduring power of attorney for property

An enduring power of attorney for property lets you appoint somebody else to act on your behalf in relation to your property (assets). You may allow your attorney to have full or partial control over your assets. You decide whether your enduring power of attorney for property should come into effect immediately, at a specific time, or only if you become mentally incapable. As long as you are capable of doing so, you can cancel or change the conditions of your enduring power of attorney for property at any time.

Enduring power of attorney for personal care and welfare

An enduring power of attorney for personal care and welfare means that someone can make decisions about your day-to-day personal care and wellbeing if you can't look after yourself. This could be because of serious illness or accident. An enduring power of attorney for personal care and welfare only comes into effect if you become mentally incapable.

When should you set up enduring powers of attorney?

Incapacity can happen for a wide variety of reasons at any time and at any age, perhaps through illness or an accident. You could also be 'incapacitated' in the sense that you are unable to act on your own affairs if you went overseas for business or decided to travel. In your absence, some urgent matter, such as signing sale documents for your property, may be required. There are numerous instances where enduring powers of attorney have saved time and additional costs – they are not restricted to older people.

Who do I appoint as my attorney?

Only an individual over 20 years of age can be appointed as your personal care and welfare attorney. Typically, it would be a family member or friend that you trust implicitly to look after your best interests. Some people have a back-up in case their attorney dies or can't perform the role. An example may be appointing your partner and a close family friend as a back-up. For your property attorney the same would apply, except that you can use an organisation to be your attorney. If you feel that your family or friends would not act impartially and in your best interests, or don't have the time or expertise to manage your affairs properly, then using a professional attorney would be preferable.

What will happen if you don't appoint enduring powers of attorney?

If you are unable to act on your affairs for any reason and you don't have enduring powers of attorney, no one can step in and manage your affairs without first applying to the Family Court. In the interim, until someone is appointed by the Family Court, your financial position could be severely affected, which may result in personal financial loss. If, for example, you had a business and were the sole signatory, no one else would be empowered to sign on your behalf and this could have severe consequences for your business, your staff and so on.

Harry was 87 years old with a number of health issues. He was also starting to suffer from mental problems. It was becoming more challenging by the day for his wife Sandra, who was a similar age, to look after him. Sandra decided she couldn't really care for Harry properly and talked to him about moving into a care facility. Needless to say, Harry wasn't very impressed and swore he was not going to leave his home. Eventually Sandra had to make the decision to go to court and get an order to place him in residential care. Not only was this a very costly exercise, it was also very stressful. If Harry had had a personal care and welfare enduring power of attorney in place, a doctor's certificate would have enabled Sandra to make the decision to get Harry the professional care he needed.

Enduring powers of attorney and wills are essential documents to have to ensure you minimise some of the risks you could face. They are easy to prepare and are a quick and inexpensive way of having proper legal plans in place for the ongoing management of your affairs. Discuss your options with your lawyer or a public trustee company such as the Public Trust or Guardian Trust.

Funeral trusts — lightening the burden for those left behind

If you are concerned about not having enough funds in your estate, a funeral trust puts money aside to pay for your funeral expenses. Rather than adding to the stress and anxiety that comes with your death, your loved ones are assured that the costs of your funeral will be covered to the amount set aside in your funeral plan.

You can choose how much you want to set aside to cover your funeral. Currently, funeral trusts to the value of $10,000 are exempt from asset testing. The funds for your funeral are invested until they are needed to pay for your funeral expenses and can not be withdrawn within your lifetime. They are available immediately when your funeral expenses are required to be paid.

There are basically two main options for putting money aside for a funeral:

1. *Savings Plan*: This is a drip-feed option where you would put aside a monthly amount until you reach the amount you want to set aside. Typically, people in their forties to fifties go for this option.
2. *Lump Sum*: This is based on your current age and how much you want to set aside for your funeral. This option is mainly used by those over 65.

What does a funeral cost?

Generally a funeral costs from $3000 upwards and the main expenses are:

Funeral Director	$750–$1500
Casket	$500–$5000
Burial	$500–$1100
Cremation	$200–$550
Plaques/headstone	$500 upwards
Plot	$550–$2000
Flowers	$100 upwards
Newspaper notices	$100–$400
Service donation	$75–$100
Total	$3200 upwards

Source: Guardian Trust

Family trusts — planning for today and tomorrow

Many people are concerned that their assets will be lost to unwanted claims, either while they are alive or through their estate when they die

– particularly since the new provisions of the Property (Relationships) Act 2002 came into force (see page 126).

Trusts are one of the oldest legal structures used to protect beneficiaries and assets, and can offer greater estate-planning flexibility and protection than a will. A trust can allow you the enjoyment and benefits of your assets without the complications and risks of owning them.

A trust is a legal arrangement whereby the trustee, as legal owner of the assets, holds assets for the benefit of beneficiaries. In simple terms, you, as the settlor of the trust, pass assets over to a trustee who becomes the legal owner of the assets. The trustee holds the assets in trust for the benefit of beneficiaries, as set out by you in the trust deed.

What are the advantages of a trust?

◇ A properly established trust can not be contested in the same way as a bequest under a will. A trust gives the settlor greater certainty that his/her wishes will be implemented.

◇ Difficulties with the combining and distribution of matrimonial property can be avoided through the use of trusts.

◇ Trusts can provide a certain level of protection from creditors.

◇ Depending on how the trust's income is distributed there may be some tax savings available.

◇ A trust may offer a protection should estate duty be reactivated or if capital gains tax is more widely implemented.

◇ Certain trusts can be set up for a specific purpose (e.g. education) and must be used for that purpose.

◇ A trust may exempt assets from current and future asset testing.

Many people have set up family trusts in the last few years but a significant number have not been administered or managed correctly. Setting up family trusts can be quite complex and the subject is beyond the scope of this book. If you think that a family trust may be of benefit to you it is essential that you seek specialist advice.

What's mine is mine and what's yours is mine!

The amendments to the Property (Relationships) Act 1976 of February 2002 mean de facto and same-sex relationships of three years or more are subject to the same rules as married couples. All property is divided equally, unless there are extraordinary circumstances.

Couples may be able to contract out of the Act if they don't want everything split down the middle. Both parties must get separate legal advice and properly drawn-up documents to this effect must be signed.

If you are in a relationship and division of property is an issue to you, it's best to plan ahead and seek legal advice. Some people think it's a bit gloomy worrying about the break-up of their relationship before they have gone too far into it. However, if it all goes sour you will be eternally grateful that you had a written agreement. If you live happily ever after, all you have lost is a few hours of your time and a couple of hundred dollars discussing future scenarios with your lawyer.

In concluding this chapter, check whether your estate planning is up-to-date and appropriate for your circumstances. If it is not, I encourage you to take action and sort it out today – as tomorrow may be too late.

In a nutshell

- ☆ Have your affairs in order by having:
  - – an up-to-date will
  - – powers of attorney.
- ☆ Will a funeral plan be beneficial to you?
- ☆ Have you looked into whether you need a family trust?
- ☆ If you are in a de facto relationship, have you addressed asset-ownership issues?

10

Building your pot of gold

Success seems to be connected with action. Successful people keep moving. They make mistakes, but they don't quit.

Conrad Hilton

The two best times to start saving are 10 years ago and today.

Anon.

The philosophy of the rich versus the philosophy of the poor is this: the rich invest their money and spend what is left, the poor spend their money and invest what is left.

Jim Rohn

If you keep doing what you've always done, you will always get what you've always gotten.

John C. Maxwell

One reason it's so hard to save is that our neighbours are always buying something we can't afford.

Anon.

The secrets of investing

Sorry to disappoint you but I don't believe there *are* any secrets of investing. Every year, though, millions of people around the world continually buy books, CDs, go to seminars, and so on, in a quest to find out the secrets of investing. In fact, these secrets are quite simply a number of basic principles:

① Start early

I cannot begin to stress enough how important it is to start as soon as possible. If I had a dollar for every time someone said to me that they wish they'd started saving in their twenties, I would have one very big pile of cash. Ideally, you should work towards saving a minimum of 10% of your income for your entire working life. If you are way past your twenties, don't panic and think it's too late or there's no hope for you – just make a decision to start today, no matter how little you are starting with.

② Pay yourself first

Most of us spend what we have. As soon as you get paid, transfer part of what you earn directly into your savings or investment account. The saying 'Out of sight, out of mind' rings true here. One could argue that the reason why most countries have a pension is because the government figured out a long time ago that people can't budget. The government takes part of its earnings and invests it every year to create a fund from which the pension is paid. Unfortunately, it's generally a pretty minimal amount, so if you want to improve your quality of life in retirement then you need to create your own fund.

As mentioned above, the target is to save a minimum of 10% of what you earn throughout your working life. The later you start saving, the higher this target needs to be. Work with your budget to ensure you have this amount available from your income. The next chapter will cover working out how much you will need.

③ Time in the market, not timing

Think long-term. Far too many people try unsuccessfully to time the market. 'Time in the market, not timing', is the common saying. What this means is don't wait for the best time to invest. Markets can be quite unpredictable and even the most experienced gurus struggle to get their timing right. Typically, they work on a philosophy of as long as they get it right more times than they get it wrong, they are doing okay. This doesn't give the average person much hope of being successful with their timing though. I read an article in the *Chicago Tribune* a couple of years ago that said that, according to their research, approximately 90% of day traders lost money. (Day traders are investors who try to make money buying and selling shares by timing the market.) Investment markets can be quite volatile, particularly in the short term, so keep focused on the long term and don't try to time the market.

④ Invest, don't gamble

To invest in something, you usually have a reasonable idea, based on factual information, that you will get a return over a period of time. Gambling, or speculating, can be very risky and usually requires a lot of skill and expertise, and isn't for the average person. Let's look at some examples:

Investing – You buy a managed fund of New Zealand-based companies, run by a known investment company.

Gambling – You buy a share in an oil company based in Argentina because you have heard that there is an oil shortage and the prices of these shares are going to dramatically increase.

Investing – You buy a rental property in a reasonably sized city or town which you know you can rent out for a certain amount per week; there is good demand for rentals, and it will gradually increase in value over time.

Gambling – You buy a property off the plans in a new resort area, because the real estate agent tells you the area is going to boom. Your plan is to sell quickly and make a profit.

Gambling or speculating can be okay, provided you accept the risks associated with it. There are often higher returns, but there is also more potential to lose money.

⑤ Have an investment strategy that suits your risk appetite

Everyone has a different attitude to risk. In my experience, approximately 80% of people fall into an average risk category. They can accept a certain amount of risk, and can cope if their investments drop in value occasionally, as long as it's not too great a drop for too long. They don't necessarily want huge returns but want a more consistent, safe strategy. It's important to know how you feel about risk. People become more accepting of risk when markets are strong, but when the markets are weak they find themselves suddenly far less tolerant of risk than they thought. If you can't sleep at night if your shares drop in value at all, you shouldn't invest in them. If you can't deal with tenants not paying their rent or trashing your property (it's bound to happen at some point), then don't buy an investment property. If you can sleep at night owing lots of money (investment debt), then building an investment portfolio may suit you. If you are a conservative investor, stay away from private equity. Some of these things may seem obvious to you, but when markets are strong people rarely think of the downside, and when the markets are weak, people tend to get consumed by them. A good investment advisor can be invaluable when helping you work out what type of investments will suit your needs.

⑥ If it sounds too good to be true it probably is!

Stay away from get-rich-quick schemes. The number of people that get caught up with various scams is actually quite astonishing. I don't know if you get as many emails as I do with pleas from Nigerian royalty promising you extraordinary amounts of money for your help in getting their funds out of Nigeria (or elsewhere in Africa). Now you may laugh, but there is an extraordinary number of people who have had their fingers burnt believing these promises. (You also have to ask yourself why the scammers would spend so much time writing and sending their emails if it didn't work.) Another common scam, which often targets high-earning professionals, is so-called stock brokers, based in Asia, calling to offer some fantastic share whose price is about to go through the roof – but for this opportunity of a lifetime you must invest immediately before it's too late. Remember, if it sounds too good to be true, it probably is!

⑦ Keep it simple

Keep your investment strategy as simple as possible. The more complex it is, the harder you will find it to understand and therefore manage. A key component of successfully building a savings fund is to keep doing it consistently over a long period of time. If you find it takes too much time to manage your investments you won't do it. If you find it too hard to understand you will also keep putting it off. Keep it simple and keep at it.

⑧ Be patient

It takes time. When talking to clients about putting an investment portfolio together for them, I like to encourage them to think at least 10 years ahead. Almost all investments have cycles. Typically they go up, they may go sideways for a while, and they may go down before they eventually go up again. Over the long term, investments should go up in value. Ten years should smooth out the effects of market cycles.

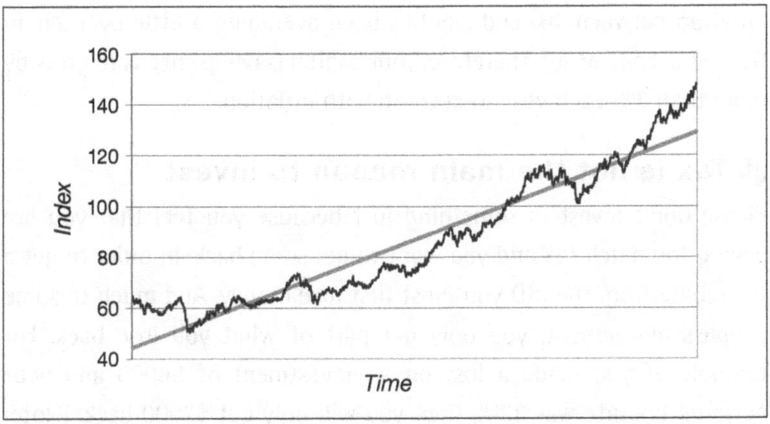

⑨ Don't overreact to short-term fluctuations

Research in America has indicated that the people who invest for the long term have received higher returns than those who invest short term or try to time the market. This is simply because investors have a tendency to buy when the market is high (when everyone is talking about what a great investment something is), and sell when the market is low or not performing well (when everyone is talking about what a lousy investment something is).

When an investment goes down in value, take a deep breath and ask yourself why you purchased that investment in the first place. If that reason is still there then hold onto it and ride through what tends to be, in most cases, a short-term fluctuation. It may even be a good idea to continue buying at 'sale' prices.

⑩ Always reinvest the interest

Always, always, always reinvest any income you receive from your investments (unless, of course, you are in retirement and living off the interest of your investments). If you invest $10,000 and spend the income from that $10,000, your investment will always be $10,000. This is a problem because of inflation. Inflation, over time, erodes the value of your $10,000. This means that in, say, 10 years' time your $10,000 will buy much less than your $10,000 today. You want to ensure that your money grows over time by more than what inflation increases by.

One of the key tasks of the Reserve Bank in New Zealand is to keep inflation between 1% and 3% (it's been averaging a little over 2% in the last decade or so). Therefore, your capital (savings) needs to grow by more than 3% each year to keep up with inflation.

⑪ Tax is not the main reason to invest

Please don't invest in something just because you feel that you are paying too much tax and you want to get some back. In order to get a tax rebate from the IRD you must first *lose* money. And much to some people's amazement, you only get part of what you lose back. For example, if you made a loss on an investment of $6000 and your personal tax rate was 33%, then you will only get $2000 back. (Note:

This doesn't apply to managed funds in respect of your personal tax return.) Losing a dollar to get a third back is a lousy reason for making an investment. However, depending on the circumstances, it can be an added bonus, particularly with property investment (see *The Complete Guide to Residential Property Investment in New Zealand* by Lisa Dudson and Andrew King or *Tax* by Martin Hawes for more detail). Accountants who tell people to buy an investment property, or business owners to buy new cars, because they are paying too much tax drive me nuts. Isn't it about *making* money?

⑫ Keep your emotions out of your investing

◇ I liked the look of the property so I thought it would be a good investment.

◇ I really like the products that ABC company makes so I bought their shares.

◇ I'll just wait until they get back up to $5 again before I sell my shares. (What happens if it takes 25 years?)

◇ My neighbour said they were a good buy.

◇ Everyone else seems to be buying them.

Do these statements sound familiar? Do you think they are good solid reasons to buy an investment or are they based on emotion? Emotion plays a big part in the way people invest. Successful investors learn to invest on the numbers and facts *not* emotion.

⑬ Work with an expert or become one yourself

If you can start saving 10% of your income from a very early age into a long-term savings plan you will develop a reasonable sum of money for retirement. If you leave it much later, you will most likely need some help. Far too many people take advice from their friends and family about investments, which I believe is often a case of the blind leading the blind.

In New Zealand today, approximately half of all adults have either negative net worth, or by the time they've cashed up they have almost no net worth. Throw in the fact that for most New Zealanders the government pension is their only source of income in retirement (about $250 per week if you are single), and you have to ask yourself if you are getting good advice from your friends and family!

You either have to seek professional advice (see Chapter 12) or you need to learn to become an expert yourself. Ask yourself if the person you seek advice from is qualified to give that advice.

⑭ Structuring your investments

There are a number of structures (trusts, companies and so on) which can hold your investments for you. These structures can offer a number of tax and other benefits for you depending on your situation. This is an area which you need to discuss with your lawyer and accountant.

The eighth wonder of the world

The power of compounding interest is possibly the most understated concept when investing. Compounding interest is simply earning interest on interest. It was Albert Einstein who said that compounding interest was the greatest force in the universe and the eighth wonder of the world.

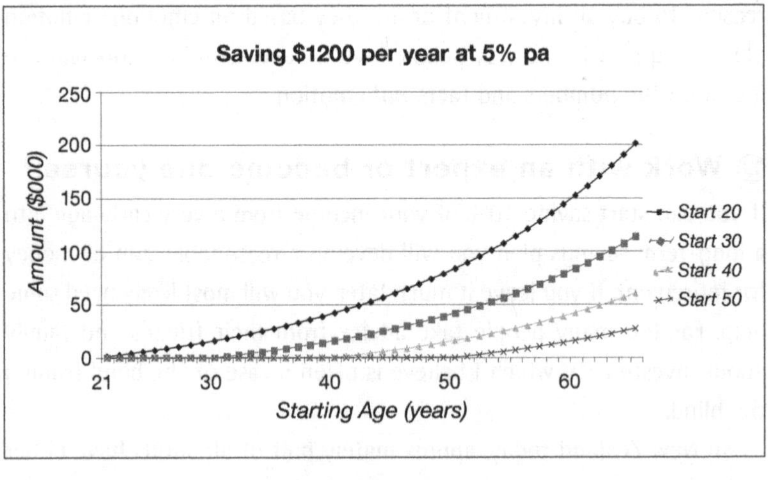

> ***Did you know?***
> Over 800,000 New Zealanders own less than $20,000 in assets.

Investors have different requirements depending on their investment timeframe. Those with longer timeframes can afford to hold a riskier portfolio, and are less likely to require income-generating investments. The asset allocation between income and growth assets is an important one. As a general rule of thumb, the younger and more aggressive you are, the more growth assets you will have. As you get closer to your retirement years, or if you are a conservative investor, you will have fewer growth assets.

How long will it take to double your money?

The 'Rule of 72' states that if we divide the number 72 by an investment's annual rate of return after tax (i.e. the net return), we will get the number of years it will take the investment to double in value. How does it work?

- ◇ If we put our $5000 in an investment that earns an annualised return of 6%, our $5000 will be worth $10,000 in 12 years (72 divided by six).
- ◇ If we put our $5000 in an investment that earns an annualised return of 12%, our $5000 will be worth $10,000 in just six years (72 divided by 12).

Work-based superannuation

Years ago, if you worked for any government organisation or large company, you would be almost certain of having a superannuation scheme as part of your salary package. However, the number of these organisations offering such schemes today has declined substantially.

Although there has been a bit of a resurgence lately. If the organisation you work for has a scheme, you should seriously consider taking it up, at the very least as a compulsory way of saving. If your company offers to match your contributions (usually up to 5%), and the scheme is run by a reputable organisation, you would be mad not to participate in it.

Savings vs investing

I have used the terms saving and investing interchangeably. Essentially they are the same thing – however, be mindful that I am referring to long-term savings. If you are saving up for a holiday, a car or a major purchase, it's quite different to long-term saving or investing, which is more for the purposes of retirement funding or replacing income from your job or business at some point in the future.

Lastly . . .

Please be patient, there are no short cuts or quick, simple ways to make you rich overnight. Follow the basic principles outlined above and you will become one of the 5–10% of people that are financially comfortable in retirement. Remember that time is one of your most powerful tools, so start today.

In a nutshell

- ☆ There are no secrets to becoming wealthy.
- ☆ Developing a good savings or investment plan is about following simple strategies.
- ☆ Time and consistency are the keys.
- ☆ Don't put it off, start today.

11

The retirement marathon

Retirement at 65 is ridiculous.
When I was 65 I still had pimples.

George Burns

The government will look after me in retirement.
And I also believe in the Easter bunny and the tooth fairy.

Anon.

Choice, not chance, determines destiny.

Anon.

It's not that I like money so much,
it's just that I find it soothes my nerves.

Joe Louis

If we did all the things we were capable of doing,
we could literally astonish ourselves.

Thomas Edison

It's all Bismarck's fault

Why do we retire at 65? The number of years you are likely to live in retirement has doubled in just a few decades. If you retired during the 1970s you could expect about 10 years in retirement before you passed away in your mid-seventies. This figure quickly rose so that if you retired during the 1990s, you can now expect about 15 years in retirement. Those of you who will retire in the 2010s are predicted to live between 20 and 25 years in retirement. What does this mean? Quite simply that you will need a lot more money during retirement than you used to if you don't want a deterioration in your standard of living.

The retirement age of 65 is actually quite arbitrary. Bismarck, considered the founder of the German Empire and Germany's first chancellor, introduced it in 1880 at the same time he introduced the world's first state pension. He deliberately chose 65 because the average life expectancy of a German at the time was just 45 years. It has already been proposed by the Australian government that the age for qualifying for a state pension be progressively increased to 70 – a view shared by a number of other modern nations as well. I would expect that the New Zealand government will also be moving towards this in the not-too-distant future.

How much is enough?

I know, I know, you will never have enough money! To live comfortably after you retire though, you have to be realistic about how much you will require. Generally, these days, people retire around the age of 65. Those who have done well financially may retire a lot earlier. However, more and more people are choosing to continue to work after 65, partly because of financial reasons or simply because they enjoy it.

Did you know?

Approx 63% of those over the age of 65 earn less than $15,000 per year.

Assuming you retire around 65, you could expect to live another 20–25 years, or maybe longer. Years ago, when people retired they became extremely attached to their recliner chairs and the television programme guide. These days, we are an active bunch and are doing so many more things in our retirement years. It's the stage in our lives where we have the most amount of time and typically the least number of commitments or responsibilities. In order to enjoy this time to its full potential you must start planning today for how much money you are going to need to live comfortably.

What sort of lifestyle do you want in retirement?

You probably don't want to lower your standard of living when you retire – after all, you won't want to stop eating and drinking out, taking holidays, buying clothes, visiting friends or relatives, or enjoying yourself in other ways. In the table on the next page write down a list of all the things you want to do and estimate what they will cost you.

What usually costs less

- Housing – you should have paid off your mortgage
- Costs of looking after children
- Travel costs to and from work
- Clothes – no need for work clothes

What usually costs more

- Medical insurance and expenses
- Home maintenance as your house gets older
- Hobbies
- Utility bills because you are at home more
- Travel, holidays

Item	Cost ($)

You can use a general rule of thumb to estimate how much you will need, which is your current income x 80%. So if you are earning $50,000 a year you will need approximately $40,000 pa when you retire. This rule is helpful to use when you are in your twenties or thirties, as 65 is too far away for you to get your head around how much you are going to need. Once you get into your forties you should have a better idea of what your retired life might look like and can work to a more accurate model by itemising your costs.

How much do you want to leave for your beneficiaries?

There are not too many people today who want to keep all their assets intact to pass on to their children, relatives or other beneficiaries. Some want to spend all their investment assets and then leave the family home as an inheritance, others want to spend every cent. Some people want to leave an inheritance to their children so they can help them out.

I would suggest that you are better off teaching your children how to manage their own money well than leaving them an inheritance when they are in their fifties or sixties (assuming you live into your eighties). Besides, it's *your* money and I am sure that after all your hard work saving it you would like to enjoy it. It's important to know what you would like to do with your assets so you can manage your estate more effectively.

Trading down the family home

I think this concept deserves a mention here. Kiwis *love* their homes. Unfortunately, we have a tendency to have all of our money tied up in them, with few other assets. In other words, we are a nation that is becoming very asset rich and cash poor. But our homes do not provide us with an income – it's cash we need to live on.

Many people I have spoken to over the years have said that they are happy having all their money tied up in their homes, because when they stop working they will trade down by either buying something smaller or moving to the country.

The reality is that they find this extremely difficult to do. Please be very realistic when considering this as a good strategy for retirement. I would argue that it is rarely effective.

There are products available that will release money from your home, but I would suggest you reserve these as a back-up plan rather than something to rely upon.

Current after-tax rates of New Zealand superannuation

The New Zealand superannuation rates aren't flash and won't allow you to live comfortably if it's your only source of income. It is important that you get a feel for how much they are though. Most people under around fifty have no clue what they are. When I tell someone that government superannuation is around $16,000 pa for a single person, typically their mouths drop and they exclaim 'Is that all?'. When I ask what they thought it was, the reply is usually 'I had no idea, but I thought it was much more than that'.

Status	Per week (net)	Per year (gross)
Single (living alone)	$318.12	$19,425.12
Single (sharing)	$293.65	$17,814.16
Couple (both qualify)	$489.42	$29,184.48
Couple (only one partner qualifies)	$465.48	$27,649.44

Source: Ministry of Social Development. Reflective of current net rates as at 14 April 2010. These figures are intended as a guide only.

> ***Did you know?***
> By 2051 there will be 300,000 women and 200,000 men over 80 years of age in New Zealand.

How long will your money last in retirement?

When you reach retirement you may want to change the make-up of your investment portfolio and make it more conservative. When you are younger, are still earning and have time on your side, you can afford to take on more risk with your investments. When you get into retirement you won't necessarily have the same earning potential so you will want to have less risk. Typically, pre-retirement your primary focus is on capital appreciation (growing the value of your investments), and post-retirement your primary focus is on capital preservation (protecting and maintaining the value of your investments).

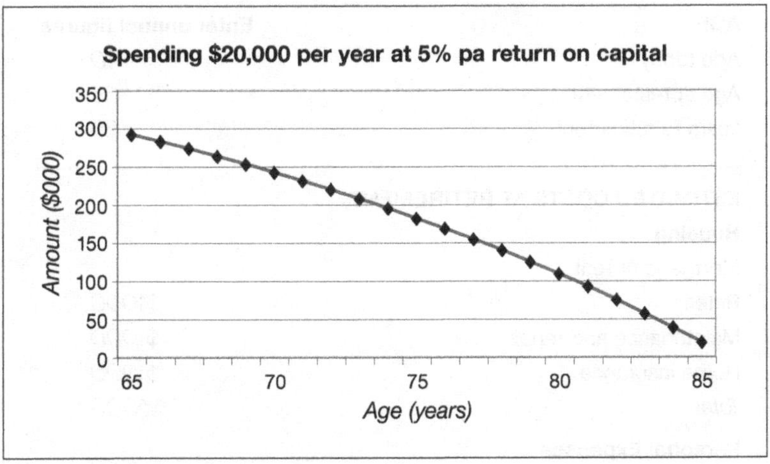

Inflation's bite

Inflation is a factor you need to consider when planning how much you need for your retirement budget. Inflation is the gradual increase in the cost of living. It erodes the purchasing power (the amount a dollar will buy) of your money. The Reserve Bank of New Zealand has the task of aligning its monetary policy to keeping inflation between 1–3%. The table below gives you some estimates to work with.

The Rule of 72 was mentioned in the previous chapter in relation to saving; however, we can also use it to work out how many years it will take for prices to double. For example, if the rate is 2%, then it will take 36 years for prices to double; if it's 3% it will take 24 years.

$$\frac{72}{\text{current inflation rate}} = \text{number of years until prices double}$$

Here is a template that you can use to work out how much you need to save each month. An example is given below. A blank template appears on pages 146 and 147.

AGE	**Enter annual figures**
Age today	40
Age at retirement	65
Years to retirement	25
ESTIMATED COSTS AT RETIREMENT	
Housing	
Mortgage or rent	
Rates	$1000
Maintenance and repair	$1000
Home insurance	$1000
Total	$3000
Personal Expenses	
Grooming	$600
Clothing	$2000

Vacations	$5000
Other	
Vehicle expenses	$2000
Vehicle insurance	$500
Total	$10,100
Living Expenses	
Groceries	$7000
Entertainment	$3000
Utilities	$1800
Telephone	$2000
Total	$13,800
Medical Expenses	
Prescription drugs	$500
Medical insurance	$2500
Total	$3000
RETIREMENT INCOME SOURCES	
Superannuation	$12,951
Company pensions	
Other retirement plans, family trust income	
Total	$12,951
SUMMARY	
Annual retirement income required	$29,900
Estimated Super, pension, and other income	$12,951
Annual income shortfall	$16,949
Enter amount already saved for retirement	$30,000
Enter expected interest rate return before retirement	5%
Enter expected interest rate return during retirement	3%
Expected years in retirement	30
Residual amount left for your beneficiaries	$100,000
AMOUNT REQUIRED FOR RETIREMENT	$376,550
Amount required to save each month until retirement	$457

AGE	**Enter annual figures**
Age today	....
Age at retirement	....
Years to retirement	....
ESTIMATED COSTS AT RETIREMENT	
Housing	
Mortgage or rent	....
Rates	....
Maintenance and repair	....
Home insurance	....
Total	....
Personal Expenses	
Grooming	....
Clothing	....
Vacations	....
Other	....
Vehicle expenses	....
Vehicle insurance	....
Total	....
Living Expenses	
Groceries	....
Entertainment	....
Utilities	....
Telephone	....
Total	....

	Enter annual figures
Medical Expenses	
Prescription drugs	....
Medical insurance	....
Total	....
RETIREMENT INCOME SOURCES	
Superannuation	....
Company pensions	....
Other retirement plans, family trust income	....
Total	....
SUMMARY	
Annual retirement income required	....
Estimated Super, pension, and other income	....
Annual income shortfall	....
Enter amount already saved for retirement	....
Enter expected interest rate return before retirement	....
Enter expected interest rate return during retirement	....
Expected years in retirement	....
Residual amount left for your beneficiaries	....
AMOUNT REQUIRED FOR RETIREMENT	....
Amount required to save each month until retirement	....

It's important to understand how inflation affects your retirement savings. If you want to have a nest egg that will give you $20,000 of income (i.e. buy you what $20,000 will today), then you need to work out how much your $20,000 needs to be at retirement time. To give you a simple example, let's assume that inflation is averaging 3%, then we know that in 24 years that $20,000 will need to be $40,000 to buy you what $20,000 will buy you today. Therefore, if you are 41 and are looking at retiring in 24 years at age 65, then you will need to have saved up enough capital to give you an income of $40,000 per annum, which effectively will buy you what $20,000 will today.

In a nutshell

☆ Planning your financial future is planning for retirement – and having the money to enjoy it.

☆ Be aware of how much the government superannuation will contribute to your retirement costs.

☆ Don't leave it until you actually retire to work out how much you will need.

12

Keeping yourself on track

To live your life in your own way,
To reach for the goals you have set for yourself,
To be the you that you want to be – that is success.

Anon.

I am a great believer in luck and find
the harder I work, the more I have of it.

Thomas Jefferson

People become really quite remarkable when they start thinking that they can do things. When they believe in themselves they have the first secret of success.

Norman Vincent Peale

Success is the good fortune that comes from aspiration, desperation, perspiration and inspiration.

Evan Esar

When it becomes all too hard!

There may be times when you'll find it all too hard and you'll wish you had never made the commitment to be a good money-manager. You wouldn't be human if you didn't have these feelings. However, the most important thing is to keep taking those small steps every day. Here are some guidelines that may help:

① Don't panic

This is the cardinal rule in all situations when it all gets a bit much. Take a deep breath and don't make any rash decisions.

② Remember your vision

Imagine yourself achieving your dreams. Remember your carrot.

③ Find some help

Who can you talk to?

④ Stay positive

Worrying about things that have already happened won't achieve anything apart from wasting energy. Focus on the future and plan for it.

⑤ Don't beat yourself up

We are only human and we all make mistakes. This is how we learn. Often it's the most successful people who have made the most mistakes.

⑥ Damage control

What went wrong? What do you need to do to get back on track? Look at your options and calmly go about putting changes in place.

⑦ Move forward

Remember, success comes one step at a time. Review your goals and reset new ones. Use your affirmations to keep you focused.

Did you know?

65% of New Zealanders get their financial advice from friends and family. A similar number of people earn less than $15,000 per year after age 65. Is this a good place to get advice?

Finding the right advice

A doctor looks after your personal health, a dentist your teeth, a lawyer your legal needs and a counsellor your relationships. But who cares for your financial health? You can either decide to do it yourself and become knowledgeable in financial matters, or perhaps it's time to consider using a financial advisor to help you achieve your financial goals.

Not all advisors are created equal, so how do you find one that best suits *your* needs. A good place to start is by asking friends and colleagues for recommendations. I am a big fan of interviewing your potential advisors just as you would if you were hiring someone in your business. You will probably be working with your advisors for a number of years, so you need to do your homework. Here are some questions you can use to help you find the right advice – they apply not only to a financial advisor but to just about any advisor you may require:

Questions to ask potential advisors:

- ◇ What qualifications do you hold?
- ◇ What is your role with the company and who owns it?
- ◇ How long have you been involved in your field?
- ◇ What practical and professional experience do you have?
- ◇ What industry bodies or associations do you belong to?
- ◇ What do you charge for an initial consultation?

- ◇ What are your other services and their associated fees?
- ◇ What types of services am I entitled to receive if I become a client of your company?
- ◇ How do you handle client money? Do you use a trust account?
- ◇ Do you have professional indemnity insurance?

Once you have the above information you can make an informed decision. Remember that deciding on the basis of fees alone can sometimes turn out to be a false economy.

Most importantly, do you like and feel comfortable with the person giving advice? As an advisor I find that the more people feel comfortable with me, then the more open they are in providing more information so that I can provide better advice.

Before making that first appointment, take the time to think about the outcomes you want to achieve from the advice you seek. The clearer you are about what you want to achieve, the more beneficial the appointment will prove to be.

Annual checklist

You should review your financial position every year to see where you are at. Has your financial situation improved? If not, what do you need to do next year to get back on track? Here are some questions you should ask:

- ◇ What is your net worth? Has it improved?
- ◇ How much do you still owe on your mortgage? Can you pay more off it?
- ◇ Have you paid off all your personal debt (outside of your mortgage)?
- ◇ Are all your important documents filed correctly? Do your executors, trustees, and so on know where the documents are?

◇ Are your insurances up to date?

◇ Is your estate planning up to date? Is your will current?

◇ Do you know where you are spending your money?

◇ Have you set your new goals for the coming year?

Net worth update

This is a great table to complete because it shows you exactly how much your wealth is increasing by every year.

Year	Net worth as at 1 Jan	Net worth as at 31 Dec	Increase
2005			
2006			
2007			
2008			
2009			
2010			
2011			
2012			
2013			
2014			

(see Chapter 4 to help you calculate these figures)

Your finances are under control when . . .

You will probably have to work 30 or 40 years before you have enough money to quit your job and live off your savings. That doesn't mean you have to spend those 30 or 40 years fretting about money. True financial independence may take decades – however, you can achieve a sense of financial freedom in just a few years. Here are some signs that you have your finances under control:

◇ Shopping is no longer your favourite hobby.

◇ You're richer than your neighbours, and they haven't a clue.

◇ You save part of every paycheck.

◇ You may not make your children or grandchildren wealthy, but you've ensured they won't inherit a nightmarish financial mess.

◇ You never dread opening your credit-card bills.

◇ You could easily afford to buy a new car, but you don't.

◇ Whenever you hear about somebody with a huge house and a driveway full of new cars, you don't wonder how rich they are. Instead, you are in awe of the staggering sums they must have spent.

◇ Your retirement dreams don't hinge on beating the market or earning double-digit annual returns.

◇ Sure, you want the big house, early retirement, the fancy holidays and the kids to go to a private school, but you realised long ago that you couldn't have it all.

◇ You're appalled whenever you see somebody buying lottery tickets.

◇ You realise renovating the bathroom is a money-loser.

◇ You have all the insurance you need, and no more.

◇ You would love to sell your house and buy a bigger one. But you get queasy thinking about how much longer you will be paying off a mortgage.

◇ You never do anything just to earn loyalty points.

◇ You cringe when you think about the time you had credit-card debt and were paying 19% annual interest.

◇ Whenever people ask you for investment advice, they're almost always disappointed by your answers.

◇ Finding the best thing you can spend on loved ones is time.

In a nutshell

☆ When it becomes difficult, take a deep breath and focus on one step at a time.

☆ Get good professional advice.

☆ Use an annual checklist to keep yourself on track.

☆ Update your net worth so you can see your progress from year to year.

Last word

In conclusion, I want to say congratulations for getting to the end. (Of course, I'm assuming you have actually read the entire book and not just the last page!). You now have two choices:

1. Continue to put your head in the sand and ignore your financial problems.

2. Resolve today to start taking small steps towards achieving financial freedom.

I strongly encourage you to take action. Make use of the principles outlined in these pages to help you become financially free – whether this means simply being in control of your money or being able to afford the life you desire. Please don't just put your head in the sand and think it will all go away – it won't. I am absolutely certain that once you have worked your way through the exercises I've outlined, not only will you obtain great results, you will kick yourself for not having started sooner. Thousands of people have used these simple strategies to get control of their finances and even become wealthy. And the most exciting thing is – anyone can do it!

Take a step today towards achieving the life you desire.

All the best, and I wish you every success.
Lisa Dudson, 2005

Recommended reading list

The focus of this book was to give you a good understanding of the basics, while at the same time not overwhelming you with too much information. Below is a brief list of some of the resources that I have found useful which will help you further your own knowledge in certain areas. I have also recommended some good websites that you may like to look at.

Books

Bell, Anita. *Your Mortgage and How to Pay if Off in Five Years.* Random House, 1999.

Hartley, Anne. *The Psychology of Money: How to turn your dreams into reality.* Hart Publishing, 1995.

Hawes, Martin. *Family Trusts: A New Zealand guide.* Shoal Bay Press, 2001.

Hawes, Martin & Baker, Joan. *Get Rich Stay Rich . . . and become financially free.* Allen & Unwin, 2003.

Jeffers, Susan. *Feel the Fear And Do It Anyway: How to turn your fear and indecision into confidence and action.* Arrow Books, 1991.

Konings, Maria & Hollings, Debra. *For Richer for Poorer: A plain English guide to help sensible Kiwis get real about relationships, money and the law in NZ.* CCH, 2001.

Molloy, Andrea. *Get a Life: Simple strategies for work/life balance.* Random House, 2004.

Pearce, Robyn. *Getting a Grip on Time.* Reed Ltd, 1996.

Schulz, Lisa. *Get Rid of Your Student Loan Now.* Random House, 2002.

Tracy, Brian. *Goals! How to get everything you want – faster than you ever thought possible.* Berrett-Koehler Publishers, 2003.

Useful websites

www.sorted.org.nz
www.goodreturns.co.nz
www.retirement.org.nz
www.cardwatch.co.nz
www.fundsource.co.nz

About the author

Lisa Dudson DipBusStud, BBS, CFP

Lisa began investing when she was just 16 years old. She has always had a passion for wealth creation and is eager to share her experience. She offers practical advice for clients based on extensive industry expertise and strategies she has personally used to successfully build her portfolio of investment in shares, property and business. Lisa also calls upon her life experience when working with clients. Her background has given her a global perspective on what most people regard as challenges when achieving what they would love – financially, emotionally and business-wise. She has led a traveller's life (having travelled in over 70 countries), corporate life, self-employment, committees and boards, leadership roles, media spokesperson, business ownership and more.

A best-selling author Lisa has appeared on TV, radio and in several magazines and newspapers. She has regularly written for the NZ Herald, Sunday Star Times, YahooXtra, Women's Day and the NZ Property Magazine. Lisa is a respected and sought-after speaker who has worked with thousands of people from very diverse backgrounds and financial situations to assist them in building sustainable, long term financial and lifestyle wealth. As well as working with the well-known *Money Man TV* show providing pragmatic financial advice both on and off screen, she has also appeared on NZ Business, Breakfast, Good Morning, 60 Minutes, House Calls, TV3 News and Campbell Live and in 2009 regularly appeared on Sunrise.

Highly qualified and holding degrees in the areas of PR, Financial Planning, Marketing and Management, Lisa is also a Certified Financial Planner who has a wealth of skills and utilizes not only her professional background but also her personal experience in working with clients.

If you would like Lisa to speak at your event or are interested in our services either send us an email or more information is available on our website.

Acumen Inc Ltd
lisa@acumen.co.nz
www.acumen.co.nz

How can we help you?

Professional services

We have spent the past five years developing the best in people and systems to assist you in your financial success. We are proud of our track record and can offer you professional assistance in:

- ◇ comprehensive portfolio and investment management
- ◇ financial consultancy
- ◇ savings plan development
- ◇ budget and money management advice
- ◇ insurance solutions
- ◇ property investment.

Courses

We believe that education is **THE KEY** to long-term success for both individuals and businesses. To that end, we offer wealth education training and a range of financial and property courses for both individuals and corporates. See our website for more details or contact us at courses@acumen.co.nz. We have a number of standard workshops and can also customise programmes for specific situations.

Professional speaking services

Lisa is a much-sought-after speaker, recognised for her practical knowledge and ability to impart that knowledge to others. She is a member of the National Speakers Association and can provide keynote, seminar and workshop presentations in the following areas:

- ◇ personal financial management
- ◇ business success
- ◇ property investment
- ◇ investment strategies
- ◇ retirement planning.

Products

As part of our commitment to financial education we have a huge range of material available both for sale and for free download on our website. Visit www.acumen.co.nz.

STAY INFORMED! Subscribe to our FREE email newsletters

Get the latest tips and news to help with your wealth and financial planning as well as free offers, information on the latest courses and current success stories. If property is your thing then you can also subscribe to 'Smart Property', featuring everything from the latest property news through to hot investment opportunities.

Membership

To really stay ahead in the financial race become an Acumen 'Success Club' member. This gives you access to the members-only area of the site where you will have opportunities to purchase products at discounted rates, download many thousands of dollars worth of product **FOR FREE** and receive advance notice of new investment opportunities. As a Success Club member you also automatically enter the monthly draw for a half-hour consultation with our budgeting consultant or our property mentor. Visit www.acumen.co.nz and join the Success Club today.

Free templates

The templates included in this book are available to download on our website: www.acumen.co.nz.

Your success stories

As I travel and speak to groups, I am often thanked for the improvements people have made in their financial and personal lives through following the principles and advice I have given through my books and personal consultations. I would love to hear your own success stories.

Email me your story at success@acumen.co.nz and go into the draw for one year's Success Club membership and a free one-hour consultation with me, Lisa Dudson.